INPOWERING
LEADERSHIP

IN**POWER**ING **LEADER**SHIP

How to Lead with
Purpose, Speed, and Accuracy
Through Change and Disruption

VIJAY JAYACHANDRAN

To Ketki, for supporting me through it all,

To Mom & Dad, for showing me how to walk the talk,

To Usha, for always believing,

&

To my many inspirational leaders, for teaching me much.

CONTENTS

PROLOGUE

You walk into the gladiator arena, your heart thumping, your brow sweaty, your throat dry.

A motley crew of warriors follows you, wary of the dangers that lie ahead.

You adjust your eyes and assess the situation. The landscape is barren, with no place to hide. Your opponents across the sand look lean and ready to fight.

The noise is deafening. Everywhere you look, there are people waving, screaming, waiting to see what will unfold.

Then a trapdoor opens, and out comes a fearsome animal you have never seen before.

This is the Colosseum, and you are in a fight for your life.

How will you get out?

INTRODUCTION

The future's uncertain and the end is always near.

– Jim Morrison, Roadhouse Blues

One of my favorite movies is "Gladiator." The protagonist is a high-ranking Roman general named Maximus Meridius, who through a cruel twist of fate loses everything and is forced to fight as a gladiator in the circus.

The movie is cinema at its grandest. When I first saw it, I was quite moved by the fight sequences where Maximus overcomes seemingly insurmountable odds to win battle after battle. I wondered how gladiators must have felt when they were thrown into the arena.

I got a visceral experience of this when I visited the Colosseum in Rome with my family. As we walked around the arena, we learned that it was built to entertain the common people and detract them from creating civil unrest.

The biggest attractions were the gladiatorial fights. The battles were medieval, bloody, and staged. As the gladiators fought to stay alive, they suddenly encountered exotic and fearsome animals they had never seen before. It was an intentional recipe for mayhem.

I tried to visualize all this from Maximus' perspective. He was an experienced soldier who had led and won many battles. He had a deep understanding of the conventional battlefield and knew how to run a strong "command and control" operation.

But the gladiator arena was very different from anything that he had experienced before. The opponents behaved in unexpected ways. The landscape was constantly changing. Maximus had to not only fight other gladiators, but also new and unpredictable animals that showed up without warning.

Then there was the noise. The screaming mass of spectators made it difficult to think and added to the overall confusion.

How did Maximus bring himself and his warriors across the finish line, again and again? How did he adapt to his new circumstances? What did he do to build a fighting unit that would persist against all the odds? Could any of his techniques be applied in our professional lives today?

THE 21ˢᵗ CENTURY BUSINESS ARENA

The imagery of the gladiatorial arena may seem far from the realities of the modern workplace. I will offer, however, that the fight for survival is metaphorically similar.

Companies and businesses today are literally in a fight for survival. As the technological landscape changes rapidly, industries are witnessing a large-scale disruption of traditional business models and operational strategies. They are attempting to survive by developing innovative products and solutions that can provide technological or business advantages against their competitors. In parallel, they are trying to do "more with less" by relentlessly squeezing costs and extracting efficiencies. They are outsourcing their products to lower-cost suppliers, offshoring work to lower-cost countries, and automating everything else with the help of computers and robots.

Small businesses are not immune to these pressures. Mom and pop shops have seen their core value propositions of "personal touch" and "responsiveness" be redefined by technologies that have replaced the front end, eliminated the middlemen, and automated large portions of the back end. Owners are adapting by becoming digitally savvy, upgrading their tools, and re-training their staff.

As businesses fight for survival, they are also being disrupted by fast-moving upstarts who challenge the status quo and play by a completely different set of rules. With angel funding and venture capital more easily accessible than ever before, startups have spawned at record rates across the globe. Unencumbered by past baggage and dogma, these newcomers are completely reimagining the customer experience. They are creating radical new solutions that provide greater convenience to customers and eliminate long-standing pain points. They have already sent numerous behemoths into oblivion, with others watching nervously from a distance, wondering when it will be their turn.

As if all of this was not enough, businesses are also having to deal with external shocks that show up with little warning and leave widespread disruption in their wake. The financial crisis of 2008 and the Covid pandemic of 2020 are two recent instances that bankrupted many companies. As these "Black Swan" events show up more frequently, CEOs are starting to ask: "What else lies around the corner? Are we adequately prepared?"

Companies, both large and small, are actively looking for help. They are engaging highly paid consultants to bring external perspectives and make recommendations. They are also hiring change agents with a mandate to "shake things up," execute radical changes, and deliver financial outcomes.

And they want everything to happen fast. Leaders know that missteps and distractions can result in a loss of time, arguably the most egregious sin in today's business environment. They have watched many established companies go from market leader to bankrupt within just a few years. They do not want to be the next one to experience this fate.

If you are in a leadership role today, you are likely experiencing some or all the above. Is it fair to say that you are feeling a little like Maximus did in the gladiator arena?

LEADERSHIP IN THE AGE OF DISRUPTION

If there is one constant in our lives today, it is change. Change itself lies on a continuum with disruption as its most extreme form. Whether it is a department-wide project, an organization-wide strategic initiative, or an industry-wide response to a Black Swan event, each creates stress and comes with its own flavor of noise and uncertainty. What kinds of leadership skills can position you for success in such an environment? That is the topic we will explore in this book.

During the Industrial Age, companies developed a hierarchical "command and control" model for managing their business. People at the top set strategy which was then flowed to the larger organization in a cascading manner. This *top-down* management model placed a premium on domain knowledge and subject matter expertise. Leaders at the top sported long tenures with significant track records of achievement. They were highly knowledgeable, self-assured, and decisive.

This operating model was successful because

business and technology cycles were long and stable. Changes happened at a slow enough pace that leaders and organizations could take their time to learn and adapt. They could afford to make mistakes, go down the wrong path for a while, and still manage to get back on track without too much long-term damage.

In recent years, the luxury to make mistakes has disappeared. The rate of structural transformation in the industry has increased exponentially, leading change cycles every few years instead of decades.

Consider that the internet took off only two decades ago, the smartphone was invented just over a decade ago, and artificial intelligence began getting to scale only in the last two to three years. The first two have *entirely* transformed how we work and live, and the third promises to soon envelop everything we do.

Rapid and radical technological changes have helped entrepreneurs reimagine how customers are served. Amazon has completely changed how we shop and driven many brick and mortar stores out of business. Online streaming services like Netflix have transformed home entertainment and are now going after Hollywood. Online travel marketplaces like Expedia and Travelocity have pretty much destroyed the travel agency business. Services like iTunes and Spotify have changed how we consume music and, in the process, eliminated the CD industry.

Apple's iPhone killed the Blackberry, then eliminated the point and shoot camera, and is now going after the secure payments business. Tesla upended the auto industry and is foraying into the power generation and storage business. Uber disrupted the taxi business, and AirBnB did the same to hotel chains.

These are just the first examples that come to mind. I am sure you can name many more.

In less than a decade, we have become intimately familiar with companies like Amazon and Netflix. In contrast, healthy and profitable brands like Sears and Blockbuster are now a distant memory. How many people accurately predicted the speed and scale of these changes?

When Jeff Bezos launched Amazon, people dismissed the online buying experience as being inefficient and impersonal. Even Bezos said at the time that he was not competing with brick-and-mortar stores. And how about Blockbuster's famous rebuff of a buyout offer from Netflix because it was a "very small niche business?" These decisions were made by smart people who had lots of experience running successful businesses. How did they get things so wrong?

The problem was that there were no good past references that could be used to guide decisions. All you could do was read the trend and decide if you wanted to jump in.

The leaders that took chances were the ones who survived. They experimented with new ideas and quickly pivoted when things did not work. When their ideas worked, they pushed on and built strong moats around their business models.

The leaders who succeeded were fast learners. They were obsessed with their customers and willing to do whatever it took to make them happy. Their clarity of purpose, dogged determination to succeed, and willingness to make hard decisions set them up for success. It also inspired their teams to come along on the journey of change and transformation.

On the flip side, some other leaders decided that there was no reason to change and continued doing business as usual. They felt secure that the barriers to entry in their industry were high, and they would have enough time to react if a competitor did something new or innovative. This had been a successful strategy for them in the past so why tinker with it?

As technological changes accelerated, however, reaction times got progressively squeezed to the point where inaction or missteps created unbridgeable gaps. The first movers ran away with the spoils while the incumbents were left behind to start a tortuous journey of de-growth followed by eventual extinction, sometimes in just a few years.

This unprecedented speed of change and disruption is not an anomaly. It is here to stay and has implications for how leaders must operate going forward. As structural changes occur every few years, it will no longer be possible to lean on accumulated knowledge or learn from mistakes over multi-year timeframes.

Indeed, the rules of the game have immutably changed. *We now live in a Volatile, Uncertain, Complex, and Ambiguous (VUCA) environment where the horizon is always fuzzy, and the scarcest commodity is time.* In such an environment, leaders must be able to learn fast and pivot quickly. They must be willing to challenge their assumptions, acknowledge knowledge gaps, crowdsource inputs when appropriate, and make radically honest and data-driven decisions.

But that is not all. Success in today's environment does not just depend on the leader's ability to evolve at a personal level. It also depends on their ability to bring their teams along with them. To move forward with speed, leaders must engage the organization's rank and file and inspire them to contribute actively. And to move forward with accuracy, they must build an environment where everyone feels heard, and the best ideas win.

Adapting to change at the individual level is already hard. Developing a culture and ecosystem where entire teams and organizations move and pivot with speed is even more challenging. This can only happen if the people trust their leader, fully comprehend their mission, and are empowered to drive action from the grassroots.

Leaders who can successfully harness the power that resides within themselves as well as their larger organizations, will be our next superstars. What changes must they execute to make this happen? Here are some thought starters.

MOVING FROM BLINK TO THINK

Society has a positive bias towards people who take quick and decisive action. We admire leaders who seem self-assured and seem always to know what to do, irrespective of circumstances. How do they do it?

In a nutshell, these leaders possess strong powers of intuition and are unafraid to use it. So, let's talk about intuition. What exactly is it?

Intuition is the ability to know something without spending time thinking about it. When we encounter a situation, our brain immediately searches for similar patterns from the past and quickly re-frames the new problem to fit into what we are already familiar and comfortable with. This *lazy brain* approach short-circuits the thinking process and helps us move forward with speed. The more experiences we have accumulated over our lives, the better is the quality of our intuition.

The book by Malcolm Gladwell titled "Blink" provides compelling examples of how intuitions (or gut instincts) can be used by everyday people to make decisions and drive successful outcomes. These examples illustrate the accuracy of snap judgments, especially in repeat situations, where past decisions can be referenced to make new ones.

Where intuitions run into trouble, however, are new and radically different situations that are unlike anything we have experienced. Because our brain is programmed to serve up intuitions, however, it still goes and finds memories that "kind of" fit the situation and entices us to use them as a reference.

There is a parable that somewhat illustrates this. A policeman sees a man frantically pacing under a streetlight. He walks up to him and asks what is going on. The man says that he has lost his keys, and they both start searching together. After some time, the policeman asks the man if he is sure that they are searching in the right place. The man replies that per his recollection, he lost the keys in the park that is just down the road. The policeman, now incredulous, asks why they are searching here instead of in the park, to which the man replies, "because there is light here, and I can see much better."

Intuition is much like this man's approach. It sheds light on things we know. Unfortunately, it is also an unconscious process that shows up, much like an uninvited guest. If we are unaware of how it works, it can drive us in the direction of familiar mental frameworks, *regardless of whether they apply or not.*

To succeed in today's fast-changing world, leaders must alter their orientation from one that always pushes for speed to one that also emphasizes accuracy. They must become more aware of their intuitions and develop ways to figure out when it is okay to *Blink* versus when they should slow down and *Think.*

The *Think* paradigm acknowledges that new and complex situations may sometimes require deeper thought and reflection. It is based on the premise that it is better to take a little extra time upfront to understand the problem and develop a solid plan than to push for quick actions and go down the wrong path.

Moving from Blink to Think can be uncomfortable for leaders accustomed to being seen as supremely knowledgeable and fully in control. When faced with an unfamiliar situation, they may prefer to rely on only a superficial understanding to make decisions. They may decide to move forward under the assumption that they can power through any issues that come up later.

Unfortunately, whenever I have witnessed this type of thinking on new or complex projects, it has resulted in continuous zigzagging without meaningful progress. With every bad outcome, the leader pushes even harder, leading to a stressful environment and long work hours. After a few painful cycles, everyone realizes that things are not working. The people in charge make some changes and re-launch the project. If the team is lucky, things get better, and they get across the finish line. If they are not so fortunate, the cycle of pain repeats.

This is not a good way to operate even in the best of times. It is a terrible way to operate when the stakes are high, and time is of the essence.

When situations feel new and unfamiliar, leaders must acknowledge their discomfort and prioritize learning over intuition. Although it does not guarantee success, it provides a higher statistical probability of achieving it.

What do leaders look like when they operate with the *Think* paradigm? They show high self-awareness, i.e., they consciously recognize when they are starting to lean on their intuition in the absence of knowledge. They have a strong nose for risk and can quickly sense when people around them are beginning to get uncomfortable. When this happens, they slow down their judgment and actively listen. They bounce thoughts with others and attempt to see things from alternate perspectives. As they collect new information, they force themselves to acknowledge what it is telling them, irrespective of how counter-intuitive it might be. This deliberate process of data accumulation and synthesis helps them gain new insights and make more accurate decisions.

It is important to note that *think* is not the same as *slow* or *inert*. "Think" requires that you make a deliberate effort to step away from your pre-programmed intuitions and seek more data in high stakes situations. This does not have to be time-consuming. It can happen fast if you quickly assemble the right resources and get their inputs. What "think" does require, however, is listening and reflection. There are no short cuts for this.

The *Think* paradigm has numerous parallels with meditation, where slowing oneself down leads to a state of calm, which in turn enables new insights. It is no wonder that many corporate leaders are embracing meditation to increase their self-awareness, manage their anxiety, and work their way through crises. These leaders have acknowledged that the world has become more complex, and their toolkit of past experiences is no longer adequate.

Once leaders adopt a learning mindset, their next challenge is to scale this up into their broader organization. If they want to be exposed to the highest quality information, they must build a culture of free speech and meritocracy where the best ideas get surfaced and heard. Let's discuss what that looks like.

MOVING FROM DIPLOMACY TO MERITOCRACY

All enterprises are somewhat hierarchical in structure, with management layers that increase in scope and level of responsibility as you move from the bottom to the top. When leaders have a decision to make, they usually listen to what their team has to say, get a couple of second opinions from trusted peers, and then make their call. The accuracy of their decision is highly dependent on the quality of the conversations that precede it.

Think back to the last time you were in an important meeting. Who attended the meeting, and how did they behave? Did the leaders come with a pre-disposition, or did they listen patiently before forming an opinion? Did the presenters meaningfully challenge their leaders, or did they tend to agree with everything they said? How did people feel after the meeting was over – were they energized and hopeful, or were they stressed and deflated?

Sometimes leaders are larger than life characters who

get accustomed to being treated with deference. They enjoy challenging others but do not like having the favor returned, especially in public settings.

These types of leaders wield a disproportionately large fraction of power in their relationship with subordinates. They create an environment where open and honest discourse is impossible. The people in their team spend a lot of time and effort "massaging" information to ensure it aligns with what their leader expects to see. And meetings become Kabuki dances, where people posture and hedge, till the leader reveals their hand. In the end, they reach a state of group think, where everyone agrees with the leader's opinion and endorses it.

Think about just how harmful this style of decision-making can be when the stakes are high. If the truth cannot easily flow upward, then organizations are effectively playing a lottery where they are betting on their leaders to pull out the winning number *all the time!*

Politics and posturing are pure waste – they can slow you down or, worse, send you down the wrong path. Meetings are not a place for leaders to show everyone that they are right. They are an opportunity for them to validate their assumptions and get critical feedback.

Leaders should put on their "listening ears" during meetings and relentlessly seek out the truth. They should work hard to create an environment where people speak up without fear, and the best ideas win, even if they are disruptive to existing plans.

In summary, leaders must evolve their culture from one of *diplomacy* to one of *meritocracy*. There are significant positives when this happens. Inclusive leaders create trust and foster a sense of camaraderie. Because people feel heard, their decisions tend to have strong buy-in, even by those not in agreement. And finally, because they are not firmly attached to their point of view and willing to accept when they are wrong, such leaders are able to pivot quickly in the face of new information.

PIVOTING WHEN CIRCUMSTANCES CHANGE

A critical decision that leaders face in fast changing environments is whether to stick with existing plans or change direction. There can be many reasons for such a decision:

- A competitor may do something that was not anticipated.

- A new technology may emerge that enables what was not feasible before.

- The regulatory environment may change, creating new risks for the business.

- A critical project may run into unforeseen challenges.

Irrespective of the reason, if leaders are unable to recognize these changes and evolve their plans quickly, they may lose valuable time and fritter away competitive advantage.

Many leaders do not pivot even when the writing is on the wall. Sometimes it is because of an innate belief that they can push through any obstacle with just a little more creativity and effort. This mentality is common and has its roots in how we are brought up.

All our life, we are taught the importance of persisting against all odds. We grow up hearing expressions like "winners never quit" and "the weak never finish." This thinking gets drilled into us during childhood and is further reinforced when we pursue our careers.

Don't get me wrong: grit and determination do work in many circumstances. If you are working on a challenging task with a well-defined path, then bull-headed determination and single-mindedness of purpose are reliable recipes for success. In fact, these are exactly the characteristics that separate you from the rest of the pack early in your career. If you show that you can stretch and push not only yourself but also your teammates across the finish line, you are sure to get noticed and promoted.

Once you start managing other people, every new success further increases your confidence. As you accumulate wins, you start to develop a belief that you can single-handedly drive success. Unfortunately, this *illusion of control* can become a problem when your path is not the right one. In that situation, no amount of grit, determination, and hard work can bring you success.

The only viable option is to pivot.

Another major reason leaders do not pivot is inertia. Once they have put an idea into motion, they are likely to keep it moving even when contrary information comes to light. Their team also plays a role in this. When they have already put effort into something, it is difficult to convince them to throw everything away and start from scratch. They feel better moving forward under the hope that things will somehow work out in the end.

Inertia is bad when you are operating in a volatile and changing environment. Instead of cutting your losses and moving on, you can end up wasting precious resources on things that no longer add value. Leaders must recognize when this is happening and pivot.

The third and perhaps most egregious reason for failing to pivot is ego. Some leaders develop an overly positive self-image as they accumulate responsibility and power. For them, being wrong in public is a horrible thing and saving face is of paramount importance. This can make them defensive about their past decisions and keep them going on a path that everyone else can see is outdated and wrong.

Losing time and opportunity due to ego is a luxury that organizations cannot afford today. When circumstances change, it is much better to acknowledge them, salvage whatever you can from the past, and change direction.

Pivoting involves stepping out of comfort zones and

taking on new and risky paths that do not have a well-defined outcome. That said, if these new paths seem the most optimal based on the data at hand, it is better to pursue them rather than keep working on things that are clearly not headed towards success.

Winners never quit, but they know when to switch. Leaders who want to win must be willing to change their plans irrespective of the inconvenience posed. That said, I will be the first to acknowledge that pivoting from a well-established plan is not easy. It is risky and puts the leader in a vulnerable spot because they are effectively second-guessing themselves. But it must be done if the situation demands it.

But wait, that's not all. Leaders must not only be able to pivot at a personal level but also get their organization to change direction with them. How can they make that happen?

BUILDING FAST AND AGILE ORGANIZATIONS

As leaders become better at learning and adapting, their next challenge is to convince their people to come along and contribute to the journey. Unfortunately, this is where many of them struggle. After doing all the hard work of analyzing the landscape and creating a roadmap, they find that their organization continues to be sluggish and indifferent. Why?

Here is a fundamental truth. When the horizon is fuzzy, people need to know where they are going and what role they will play before they can decide if they want to get on board.

Think of your enterprise as a house where you and your team live. The first question the people in your team will ask is: *Is this house stable?* In other words, is this business on solid ground? Is my job secure for the foreseeable future?

Once they feel good about this, the next question they will ask is: *Is this house growing?* In other words, is this business on a growth path? Is it a good place for me to continue investing my time and effort?

When they feel assured about this, the final question they will ask is: *Can I help grow this house?* In other words, do I have a say in my future? Am I empowered to contribute to this business's success, and am I included in the decision-making process?

If you, as a leader, have created an environment where your people answer yes to all three questions, then you are leading an engaged organization that will actively assist you in making the challenging journey through change and disruption.

When the organization is small, creating engagement is relatively straightforward. When you can fit everyone in one room, you are able to meet regularly, exchange ideas, and keep everyone on the same page.

As an organization increases in size, however, it becomes exponentially harder to keep everyone aligned and engaged. As you create management layers you also create bottlenecks. Information is lost in translation as it goes up and down the chain. As new departments get added, they can work at cross purposes with each other if the mission is not clearly defined and aligned.

Leaders of fast and responsive organizations must actively address all the above issues. They can do so by following the "Inpowering Leadership" framework.

THE INPOWERING LEADERSHIP FRAMEWORK

I wrote this book based on what I learned over my career about effective organizational leadership. I drew on my personal experiences of leading global teams and programs. I also drew from my observations of inspirational leaders who I worked with over the years.

The early days of my career were like those of many other leaders. I grew by taking on assignments with progressively increasing scope and responsibility. What was perhaps somewhat different, however, was my willingness to take on new and unfamiliar roles. I started my career in corporate research and went on to work in product development, operations, and marketing, all of which challenged and stretched me in different ways.

During my early years as a manager, I learned a few important things:

1. The world was too complicated for me to know everything. The only way to solve meaningful problems was by collaborating with other smart people.

2. I could not possibly do everything or be everywhere. If I wanted to increase my contributions, I would have to empower other people and give them end-to-end responsibility for portions of my work.

3. I could not be promoted if I was irreplaceable in my current job. To take on new and exciting growth assignments, I had to build a bench that could replace me.

These learnings shared a common theme. They showed me that *my success and growth as a leader depended on how well I could harness my team's knowledge and capabilities.*

I got the opportunity to put these learnings to the test when I went to India on a three-year expatriate assignment. The country was seen as the next big market where our competitors had introduced new and disruptive products. We would have to react with speed to maintain our dominant position in the market.

As an expat, my job was to be a change agent. I was expected to bring in new ideas and build a world-class team that would sustain itself after I departed.

I waltzed in, confident that I would quickly sum up the situation, execute decisive changes, and start delivering results. Within a few weeks, however, I came to the realization that despite my experience and strong track record, I was not equipped with the knowledge required to navigate this new environment. All my prior work experience was from the US, whereas I was now in an emerging market where customer expectations and organizational culture were quite different. I would not succeed by merely leaning on my past learnings and experiences. I would need to combine them with the local team's knowledge to develop a complete picture and create the best possible plan.

When I started, every moment felt rushed. The business pressure was urgent, and the demands from stakeholders were unending. Advice seemed to pour in from everywhere, and we were working on too many things.

To cut out the noise, we held small and focused discussions with customers, stakeholders, and team members. I also carved out solo time so that I could process my thoughts.

Over the following weeks and months, a picture started to emerge. We identified some clear priorities and developed a strategy. We discussed and aligned this with our stakeholders and our leadership chain to ensure that we would get their active support in taking the various initiatives forward.

Next, we communicated the plan to everyone in the team in a concise and understandable way. We encouraged each person to personalize the information and think about what they could do at their level to drive positive outcomes for the organization.

We held several cross-functional brainstorming workshops and launched many joint projects with different stakeholders. As the projects went forward, we maintained a regular stream of communication. I personally ran "all-hands" meetings to ensure that everyone was aware of the latest developments and any changes in priorities.

I constantly reminded everyone that we were looking for ideas and created some small awards to recognize submissions. I soon started getting visitors. People walked into my office with questions, ideas, and on occasion, piercing insights into our strategy.

I also started getting suggestions from stakeholders in other departments who saw that we were genuinely trying to help. These interactions not only brought in new thoughts but also increased overall engagement and buy-in for our strategy.

It was an eventful journey, but in the end, the hard work paid off. The products we introduced did quite well in the market and the financial metrics improved with every passing quarter. The team was recognized for its contributions and won numerous corporate awards. It did not end there – we built a set of best practices that were leveraged for further success in the following years.

After I returned to the US, I reflected on how I, along with the larger India organization, had navigated this turbulent and disruptive period. I recognized four discrete enablers that had been critical to our success.

The first was establishing an aligned *purpose* for our mission. We set a clear "North Star" that everyone could understand and use to guide their day-to-day decisions. We worked with the C-level to ensure that they bought into this North Star. We also aligned incentives to ensure that all stakeholders would work towards a common mission.

The second enabler was *speed*. We did a lot to decentralize decision-making and empower the organization to take the initiative. This created huge multipliers on efficiency and enabled us to deliver way more than would be possible in a top-down operating model. It also gave the leadership team some bandwidth to think and strategize rather than spend every waking minute in a firefight.

The third enabler was decision-making *accuracy*. We proactively reached out to all our stakeholders to understand their pain points. We solicited inputs from all parts of the organization. We encouraged people to speak up even when they disagreed with me or anyone else in the leadership chain. We learned quickly from our mistakes and pivoted when it was apparent that we were on the wrong track. All this helped reduce missteps and waste.

The fourth enabler was building organizational *resilience*. I, along with the leadership team, worked 24/7 to motivate our people even when things got rough. We visibly demonstrated energy and enthusiasm for the mission and helped everyone visualize success. We actively coached and mentored people to help them get across roadblocks. And along the way, we instituted best-in-class processes that persisted even after many of us had moved on.

These four enablers helped us build an organization that moved with purpose and delivered meaningful outcomes despite all the distractions. The experience also taught me something fundamental about leadership. It taught me that leading an organization in times of change requires more than individual brilliance. It requires an ability to get people excited about the cause and create an environment where they can shine and make a difference. It requires a leadership style that *powers people from the inside,* ignites their passion, and extracts the best out of them.

The four elements – purpose, speed, accuracy, and resilience – are the foundations of the Inpowering Leadership framework. This framework can be used by any leader to power themselves as well as their organization through difficult times.

All change events, small and large, create their unique noise and come with their own set of uncertainties. Inpowering Leaders cut through the noise by setting a clear horizon and inspiring their organization's rank and file to participate in the journey. The leadership team in India employed this exact approach to achieve success. We worked together to align around a common cause, listened to each other objectively, learned collectively, and then put in some good old-fashioned hard work to cross the finish line.

The Inpowering Leadership framework is built upon a foundation of thinking and learning. It requires a willingness from leaders as well as their people to challenge personal assumptions and honestly interpret ground realities. Its success depends on building a meritocratic environment where difficult decisions get made quickly, and pivots get executed with speed.

I have personally applied the framework many times during my career, experiencing both success and disappointment, depending on how well I executed the individual steps. I have also benchmarked this approach with peers in the industry. The feedback has been consistent – in today's world, companies that learn fast and fully leverage their knowledge and talent have the best chance to survive and thrive. The Inpowering Leadership framework provides a practical and repeatable approach for this.

The Inpowering Leadership framework

Many companies and organizations are already operating with some version of this framework. They are flattening their organization structures, fostering autonomy at all levels, making hard decisions, and moving forward with speed.

There are also many companies, however, that are operating in the old command and control construct. Their leaders are trying to do it all – interpret the landscape, develop strategy, define projects, (micro) manage people – and struggling to make meaningful progress. It seems like they are stuck, constrained by old rules and operating paradigms.

Are *you* a leader looking for ways to break out of the old construct and try something different? If so, this book might be able to help you. In the coming chapters, I will take you on a hands-on journey through the Inpowering Leadership framework and help you apply it to your specific context.

In Chapter 1, I will talk about creating clarity and focus for your organization and giving it a strong sense of purpose. We will discuss the importance of setting a North Star and how you can design an effective one. We will also discuss mission alignment across teams and up the leadership chain, a critical prerequisite for success.

In Chapter 2, I will describe how you can compound your impact and move your organization forward with speed. We will discuss mechanisms for empowering your people and creating an army of trusted lieutenants who understand the mission and work with little supervision.

In Chapter 3, I will talk about how you can open yourself up to radical learning and build a data-rich environment. We will explore techniques by which you can leverage your organization to make honest decisions and drive high-quality outcomes.

In Chapter 4, I will talk about building resilience – how you as a leader can set a positive tone, walk your talk, and inspire your team to persevere through difficult times and achieve more than they thought possible.

I will conclude with some final remarks at the end of the book.

IT'S DECISION TIME

It is time for you to make a choice. You can close this book and go back to your world with my best wishes. Or you can keep reading and come with me on a journey of personal exploration.

Before you start, I must caution you that the journey will not be comfortable. Inpowering Leadership is an inherently disruptive process. It requires you to examine your personal style and make changes to it. It requires a willingness to deviate from social norms.

If you have been set in your ways for some time, it may take much work to re-imagine yourself and put the changes into practice. That said, the journey will be worth the effort because irrespective of the outcomes, you will emerge on the other side as a better, stronger, and more self-aware incarnation of yourself.

Are you ready to take the plunge?

BECOMING SELF-AWARE

You must unlearn what you have learned.

– Yoda

Welcome curious traveler. It looks like you made the decision to keep going. I feel privileged to enjoy your trust and am excited to get started.

This chapter is a bridge to what lies ahead. It is a deliberate side journey that will make you a little more self-aware and prepare you for the conversations you will encounter in later sections.

This book is structured as a hands-on learning experience. You will encounter numerous "timeouts," where you will be expected to stop and reflect. These discrete breaks in the learning journey will help you get calibrated on specific aspects of your operating style and formulate adjustments that you can put into practice.

This approach is based on methods that I developed and used extensively over my career. It is based on the premise that *the most consequential and enduring learning only happens by doing and experiencing.* To make real changes to your operating DNA, you must go through the personal effort of formulating ideas and putting them into action, again and again.

WHO ARE YOU?

As individuals, we have a unique way of thinking and doing things that are an outcome of our genetic makeups and our experiences since birth. Our operating styles are embedded in our brains and neural pathways in the form of instincts, intuitions, and beliefs, all of which guide us in our daily lives. These inner forces define where we fall on the spectrum of introversion versus extroversion, optimism versus pessimism, risk taking versus conservatism, delegating versus micro-managing, etc. These attributes serve as strengths in many situations and can be limiting in others.

In the coming chapters, I will challenge you to examine various aspects of your operating style and decide if changes are warranted. These mental exercises will be a conversation between you and yourself. You alone will be responsible for figuring out what is working well and what could use some tweaking.

Once you have identified things to work on, you will design experiments to run in your daily life. I will support you with examples and thought starters, but you will be responsible for developing the actual experiments. This approach is based on the belief that all humans are unique, and hence their path to change must also be unique. Although I will suggest some best practices based on my experiences, the exact implementation for your context and circumstances will have to come from you.

Some of the experiments you devise will be straightforward and easy. Others will take you out of your comfort zone. It is the latter that will induce measurable change and growth.

As you try things that feel unconventional or risky, you will encounter internal resistance. Voices will show up in your head, advising you to reconsider. You may even experience physiological symptoms like sweating and nausea. Such sensations are normal. All humans are wired to protect themselves from harm, and these discomforts are just a manifestation of that protective mechanism trying to keep you out of trouble.

You will need to find a way to cut through these inner noises. You will need to acknowledge their presence, understand how they manifest themselves, and work deliberately to overcome them. Once you have done this, you will be able to think more clearly and run your experiments. As you repeatedly execute the experiments, your brain will progressively become more comfortable with its "new normal" and, over time, get rewired into a new operating style.

How can we cut through the inner noises that push

us towards safety every time we try something new? The first step is to become aware about how these forces operate and how they impact us.

In the following sections, I will introduce you to how our instincts, intuitions, beliefs, and fear of failing bias our interpretation of the world and sometimes hold us back from achieving our full potential. I will also describe techniques for overcoming these forces.

The coming discussions are not meant to be a comprehensive lesson in psychology. There are many other books that go much deeper[1]. My primary intent is to create some level of self-awareness before you embark on your journey of personal disruption.

INSTINCTS

All humans possess a set of instincts – hardwired behaviors that get activated in the presence of certain stimuli. These behaviors are already present when we are born and stay with us for life.

The most primal is our instinct for survival. Any time we feel threatened, our brain triggers a "fight or flight" response and sends our body into a heightened state of arousal. Our muscles tense, hormones get released, and blood rushes to our limbs, getting them ready to punch back or run.

---

[1] There are a few in the Selected Readings section at the end of this book.

Fight or flight is a critical instinct. In life-threatening situations, it helps us react quickly and move to safety. Unfortunately, this instinct can also get triggered when we experience extreme stress or feel personally challenged.

Imagine you are in a meeting and get directly challenged by a colleague who disagrees with you. If you are sensitive to such challenges, your survival instincts can take over and make you respond inappropriately. You can lose your temper, become unyielding on your position, and in the worst case, storm out. This type of reaction is clearly not appropriate to the situation. A better way would be to continue the conversation, dig deeper to understand why the other person is pushing back, and work together to arrive at an amicable conclusion.

But perhaps you are just more reactive than other people. In that case, can you rewire this behavior? The short answer is yes, but it takes effort. If you can train yourself to recognize when your protective instincts are getting triggered, you can attempt to deliberately slow down your response and take more time to understand the situation. This is not easy to pull off, however. It requires *a strong sense of self-awareness* and *a great deal of preparation*.

Let me illustrate with an example. All my life, I have been terrified of snakes. Whenever I encounter one, I immediately experience a visceral impulse to either harm the animal or run for my life. This is an autonomous reaction whose onset I cannot control.

Considering, however, that only 7% of snakes in the world are poisonous, my response is clearly irrational in most situations. Can I do better?

A few years ago, I decided to work on this phobia. I read up on snakes and learned about their importance to the natural ecosystem. I learned that they are way more fearful of us than we are of them. When I visited national parks, I met rangers who spoke about them with a conspicuous lack of fear and revulsion. I even met animal lovers who were comfortable handling snakes and spoke fondly about them, almost like one would talk about a pet dog or cat. Those conversations were aha (!) moments for me.

As I learned more about snakes, I started visualizing my next encounter and how I would respond. I ran small experiments, such as, when I saw a garden snake in my back yard or when I handled a boa at the petting zoo. Each time, I forced myself to be a little more logical and nonchalant. After each experience, my subliminal response got slightly rewired in the direction of goodness.

Today, I am a different person when it comes to snakes. I still experience an illogical first reaction when I see one. But now I am able to slow down, evaluate the situation, and react appropriately.

When I think back to how I got here, I can pinpoint two things. The first is *extensive learning*. By reading books and speaking with people I respected, I became significantly more knowledgeable and logical. The second is *visualization*. I performed numerous solo sessions where I relived prior experiences and planned for the next ones. This type of offline preparation helped me achieve real-time success.

Now, here is an unexpected gift. My evolution did not just stop at snakes; I was able to extend it to how I react to many other wild animals. Many years ago, my wife and I encountered a black bear along a hiking trail in Alaska. Both of us had prepared in advance how to react in such a situation and were able to retreat without panic. Shortly after, we saw another hiker cross paths with the same bear. He panicked, tried to run, slipped, and fell on the trail. Fortunately, the bear took no notice and just kept walking.

The other hiker was lucky; things could have turned for the worse quite easily. My wife and I, on the other hand, made our own luck. By being prepared, we executed a calmer response, and created a *statistically higher*[2] probability of success for ourselves.

Let's look at another example, this time from the workplace. I have always had an instinctive dislike of crowds and fear of public speaking. Although this was not an issue early in my career, it started becoming one when I started leading teams. I recall the first time I made a presentation to the CEO of our company. We had a few dry runs before the event, and I suffered a nervous breakdown during one of them. Fortunately, a

---

[2] Note that we could have still had a bad experience if, for example, the bear was injured or had babies near it.

senior leader helped me that day. He understood what I was going through and immediately disbanded the meeting. He spent the next two hours with me, understanding the material and helping me formulate an easily understandable story for each slide in my presentation.

After we were done, he said something that stuck with me. He said, "Vijay, always remember that when you are the subject matter expert, no one can hurt you on the facts. You should stop worrying about that and focus instead on creating compelling stories for your audience." The first part of his statement gave me an aha (!) moment. It made me realize that my fears were rooted in worries about looking incompetent. Once I convinced myself that I knew more on the topic than anyone in my audience, my fears melted away. I was now able to focus on *how* I was telling the story rather than *what* was in it.

From that day on, I have always prepared meticulously ahead of presentations and speeches. I first ensure that I am on top of the facts and only after that go to the next step of building a compelling story. If I am not the subject matter expert, I ensure that there is one with me, ready to take questions. This approach has helped me calm my protective instincts and become a more confident public speaker.

The above story tells us that overcoming instincts does not have to be an entirely personal endeavor; you can also bring in others to help. By honestly evaluating your innate strengths and limitations, you can bring in people with complementary skills to help you succeed.

Before we go any further, I would like you to take a short timeout. Please spend the next few minutes thinking about the questions below. Feel free to bounce your thoughts off a relative or friend who understands you well.

1. Can you list your phobias and fears[3]? Are there any that you have been trying to overcome?

2. Think of one instinctive fear that you can work on in the coming days. Do you think you could spot the situation when it occurs the next time? What steps could you take, either personally or with others' help, to adjust your reaction? Are you able to visualize the sequence of events that would play out in the old way and the new way?

Timeout

Welcome back. You just went through an exercise in personal disruption. I hope you found it revealing. I encourage you to continue thinking about the phobia you selected and actively prepare for your next encounter.

---

[3] Some common ones include fear of heights, blood, spiders, snakes, being in a confined space, and being alone.

INTUITIONS

In the last section, we discussed instincts. These are *hardwired* behaviors learned over millennia that exist in all humans at varying levels of intensity. We will now move into the world of intuitions – learnings that are accumulated during our lifetimes.

Whereas *nature* embeds a consistent set of instincts within us, *nurture* takes us in all sorts of directions. After birth, all of us go through unique developmental experiences within our families and social ecosystems. These experiences shape us in unique ways and result in a custom set of intuitions and beliefs that influence how we interpret the world around us. To evolve our operating style, we must acknowledge these subliminal forces and understand how they are impacting us.

Let us start with intuitions, also known as "gut instincts." Intuitions are based on past experiences and just like instincts, get subconsciously triggered by external inputs.

When we encounter a new situation, our brain quickly serves up a smorgasbord of similar memories. We then have a choice – we can instantly use these past experiences to guide our decisions, or slow down, analyze the situation more deeply, and only after that, make our decisions.

Unfortunately, our brain is wired to conserve energy and pushes us down the quick and lazy path. It readily serves up old memories as intuitions and entices us to make decisions based on them, *even when they are not a good fit for the situation.* All of this puts us in a tricky position. Since there is no way to know when our intuitions are right or wrong, how can we decide when we should deliberately slow down (think) versus just proceed with our gut (blink)?

Although this will always be a matter of judgment, a good way to think about it might be as shown in the decision tree below. The first question to ask when you face a new situation is: "Have I seen this before?" If it is something you have done many times before, you can simply go ahead and leverage your experience. If the situation is new, however, it is the first signal that you may want to take a step back and question what your gut is telling you.

The next question to ask is: "What is the consequence of failure?" In other words, if you get this decision wrong, will the outcome be acceptable? If not, will you be able to reverse the situation? If you feel that the consequences will be painful (such as financial loss or brand damage), you should slow down, get into the gnarly details, and force your brain to make a data-driven decision.

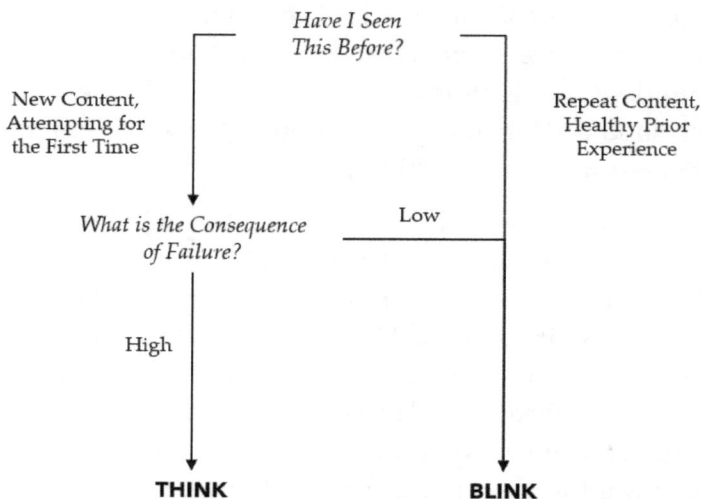

Have I Seen This Before?

New Content, Attempting for the First Time

Repeat Content, Healthy Prior Experience

What is the Consequence of Failure?

Low

High

THINK

BLINK

The Think v/s Blink Decision Framework

As you get to your decision, you should also calibrate if you are going *with* the consensus opinion or *against* it. If the latter, you should take another step back and assure yourself that you have been genuinely dispassionate and honest[4]. Once you have taken all these extra steps, you can commit and proceed.

The above decision framework is built on the premise that all decisions are not made equal. If the potential impact of making a poor decision is low, it is acceptable to keep moving, even when the situation is new and unfamiliar. On the other hand, if the potential

---

[4] Going against the grain is just a warning sign, not a showstopper.

impact is high, it is better to slow down and get a second opinion, even if you are intuitively feeling confident.

The best place to get second opinions is from people who think differently from you and have had different life experiences from yours. Such people can widen your worldview, uncover your blind spots, and provide a richer set of data to inform your decisions.

The above framework is subjective – your decision to slow down entirely depends on how *you* interpret the novelty or riskiness of the situation. It may not match what another person decides when faced with the same information. Also, the quality of your decision depends on the quality of alternate inputs you generate and how openly you listen to them. That said, the very act of going through this deliberate process should give you a little more clarity and a statistically higher chance of success.

This is a great place to stop and take another timeout. Please answer the below questions. Be honest as you answer them and act like no one is watching (because no one is).

- Think back to a critical project or initiative that ran into significant problems. How new or unprecedented was the content, and how unforeseen were the issues?

- In hindsight, were there any warning signs before things went wrong? If yes, what prevented you or the people around you from taking action?

- Can you think of any people inside or outside your organization who could have helped you prepare better? Would you be willing to solicit their input the next time you tackle a similar new problem? Why or why not?

⧖ Timeout

Welcome back. How did that exercise go? Did you identify any learnings that you could apply going forward? I hope you will try out the "Think v/s Blink" decision framework and run a few experiments in the coming weeks and months.

BELIEFS

So far, in this chapter, we have covered instincts and intuitions, two subconscious mechanisms that impact how we interpret the world and react to it. Let us talk next about beliefs – a set of openly visible traits that sometimes create their own barriers.

I define beliefs as *strongly held values and attitudes*. Beliefs are usually ingrained in us by trusted authority figures or by highly memorable and meaningful life experiences (both good and bad).

Here are some examples of beliefs: "Truth and hard work always prevail"; "People are generally good and kind"; "Everyone is in it only for the money"; "The ends justify the means"; "It is okay to do something if everyone else is also doing it"; "People never change"; "You should always put others before yourself"; "Winning is everything."

All of us are proud of our beliefs and values. We use them as a vehicle to communicate who we are and what makes us tick. We take umbrage when they are questioned and are willing to defend them under pressure. *Our beliefs define our brand.*

Can you enumerate some of your beliefs? Can you trace back to when and how you acquired them? Most importantly, do you think they sometimes limit your ability to make the right decisions?

As you chew on this, let me tell you a few things about myself. I spent my formative years in India, a country that culturally emphasizes the collective over the individual. My father was an officer in the Indian Army. He was upright, non-political, and known for the care he showed for the soldiers under his command. My mother was a patient and indulgent schoolteacher. Her defining attribute was her willingness to give anyone the benefit of the doubt.

My parents were on the liberal end of the spectrum; they gave me space and freedom to explore new and sometimes unconventional ideas. They sacrificed much to ensure that I had a comfortable life and a solid education.

Do you think my experiences as a child are impacting how I view the world and operate in it today? I am sure they are. The uneventful and happy years that I experienced as a child gave me a generally positive outlook on life and instilled a set of beliefs that emphasize the goodness of humanity. Due to this, I view certain situations with optimism when pessimistic outlooks might be more appropriate; I interpret certain actions as benign when they might be threats; I negotiate from a position of trust and sometimes leave money on the table ... I think you get the point.

Let me now offer up some experiences that I *did not* have during my childhood. I never lived in a high crime neighborhood; I never experienced a riot or social disruption; my parents never went through bankruptcy or divorce ... I hope you see the trend. My optimistic and trusting outlook has as much to do with what I *did not* experience as what I *did* experience. This combination of experiences <u>and</u> non-experiences has instilled beliefs that act as strengths in some situations and limitations in others.

Are there ways by which I can overcome limitations imposed by my belief systems? The short answer is yes, but they require *self-awareness* and a *willingness to be helped by others*. For example, if I am aware that my beliefs make it difficult for me to negotiate hard, I can enlist experts to help me during high-stakes negotiations. I can empower them to represent my interests and give them the authority to make decisions.

By doing so, I can fill a visible gap in my skillset, stay true to my beliefs, and maintain a consistent brand.

Please stop here and take a timeout to reflect on your belief systems. You may want to enlist the help of a close relative or friend. Whether you like it or not, your beliefs and values are quite visible to the people around you. Sometimes, an external perspective can be quite illuminating.

1. Think back to your formative years. Who were the people that influenced you the most? What are some of the beliefs and values you picked up from them?

2. How might your beliefs and values be impacting the way you think today? Think of both the benefits as well as drawbacks.

3. Choose one belief that is limiting you in some way today. What could you do to overcome it?

Timeout

Welcome back. How did that go? Did the exercise create visceral discomfort? Did it drain you mentally? If you answered yes to both questions, you just had a productive session. I encourage you to keep thinking about this topic and put some of your ideas into action.

FEAR OF FAILING

Now that we have understood how instincts, intuitions, and beliefs can color our judgment, it is time to discuss the inner demon that sometimes holds us back the most – our fear of failure.

Most of us care deeply about our public image. We strive to look like we are always in control and hate to try something that could fail in public. This is based on a deep-rooted behavior within us called *loss aversion* that was studied extensively by Nobel Laureate Daniel Kahneman and his colleague Amos Tversky in the 1970s. In their seminal work on Prospect Theory, Kahneman and Tversky showed that people avoid losses and prioritize wins because *the pain of losing is greater than the satisfaction of an equivalent win*. This mentality makes them averse to taking risks, not just in their personal lives, but also in their professions.

Related to loss aversion is our desire to comply with social norms and do whatever we can to fit in. All of us coexist within society by behaving in ways that are generally considered acceptable by the people around us. Although we may privately question the prevailing norms, few among us are willing to flout them publicly. This is even more true in today's world of social media, where stepping out of line can quickly render us as pariahs within our communities.

Social forces make us think twice about doing anything different and prevent us from leaving the safety of the pack. Unfortunately, if the pack provides a sense of safety, it also fosters a spirit of mediocrity. While staying in the pack can reduce the risk of social rejection, it can also deny us the growth and satisfaction we seek. It certainly cannot help us in times of change and disruption when we *must* do something different to succeed.

All of us have people in our social circles who have stepped out of the pack and achieved great things, professionally or personally. They are sometimes referred to as mavericks – brave to challenge social norms, act differently, and create a new normal. We admire such people from afar, sometimes wishing we had the strength to be like them. We stay put, however, paralyzed by fear of the unknown.

What does it take to go down the path less taken? How can we overcome our fears and change the narratives of our lives? Let me offer some ideas based on my experience.

During my career, I regularly forced myself to take on tasks and assignments that were outside my comfort zone. As I reflect on what enabled me to do this, I see three consistent themes:

1. **A solid support system**. I always had an open line of communication with my company's senior leaders who understood my aspirations and were willing to take a chance on me. Their support created a solid foundation from which I could try new things without worrying too much about losing my job.

2. **Extensive preparation**. Every time I changed direction, I did extensive research and created all sorts of hands-on experiences to climb the learning curve. The hardest part was opening myself up to learning from people who were significantly junior to me. As a leader, how would it look when I showed my lack of subject matter knowledge? Although this felt awkward, I convinced myself that my openness to learning would foster trust and create stronger relationships. I was never disappointed.

3. **Mental Calm**. I found ways to overcome the gut-clenching fear of failing and how that could impact my public image. Interestingly, having a support system and preparing extensively helped me with this. Once those were in place, I simply had to convince myself that the path I was undertaking had enough upside to make it all worth my while. I constantly visualized what success might look like and used it as a motivator to move forward.

These three ingredients provided a repeatable recipe to run experiments in my professional and personal life. I started every experiment with a sense of trepidation but always emerged stronger and happier on the other side.

These pain and reward cycles grew my resilience and increased my willingness to step out of the pack. They also helped me understand who I was and what made me tick.

As you lead your organization through change and disruption, you too will have to try new things and experiment your way out of difficult situations. Although this will feel risky, you will have to find a way to build your confidence and move forward with intent. Having a strong support system, preparing extensively, and actively calming your mind, will provide an excellent foundation to get you going.

Please stop here and take a timeout. This time, I would like you to think about your propensity for risk-taking and willingness to step out of the pack. Please be honest and genuinely explore this topic.

1. How satisfied are you with your current state – both professional and personal? Are there new and exciting things that you aspire to do but have not executed? If so, what is holding you back?

2. If there was one significant change you could make, what would that be? Could the three ingredients help you get past your obstacles?

Timeout

CHAPTER SUMMARY

In this chapter, we discussed our innate tendencies and behaviors that create blind spots and drive poor decisions. We talked about instincts, intuitions, and beliefs, all of which subconsciously impact how we think and act. We also discussed our fear of stepping out of the pack and how it holds us back from exploring our full potential.

The intent of this chapter was to make you more aware of how the above mechanisms work, how they impact you as a leader, and what frameworks you can use to analyze and overcome them. With these concepts under your belt, you are ready to explore the material that lies ahead.

As you navigate change and disruption, you will need to challenge not only the status quo *around* you but also the one *within* you. You will need to throw away many of your old rules and become comfortable with new ones. This process will make you more self-aware as a leader and prevent others from taking advantage of you. As Tyrion remarked in the Game of Thrones, "Once you've accepted your flaws, no one can use them against you."

The human brain exhibits *neuroplasticity* – an ability to be rewired through repeat experiences and deep reflection. This is interesting because it provides a pathway to reprogram our thinking and move towards a more optimal state.

In the coming pages, you will be pushed to examine your operating style and make changes to it. You will start running experiments in your daily life and use the learnings to make progressive adjustments. This will not always be easy. There will be days when you will doubt yourself and wonder if you should just stop and go back to how things were. *But you will persevere* by 1) setting up a solid support system, 2) preparing extensively, and 3) actively calming your mind. And by doing this again and again, you will permanently rewire yourself.

A QUICK NOTE ON TIMEOUTS

In the last chapter, you were introduced to the concept of timeouts. These were meant to make you stop and think about the material covered in the preceding paragraphs and develop action plans when appropriate.

There are more timeouts in the coming chapters. The amount of time you spend on them is entirely up to you.

If the material sounds familiar and you feel like you are already doing all the things it recommends, you can simply move on. If, however, you discover significant gaps in your operating style, I recommend that you stop, develop meaningful actions, and put them into play.

You may decide that you want to read the entire book first and then come back to do the timeouts. That is an acceptable approach if it feels more comfortable. You should do whatever works for you.

As you run experiments, I highly recommend that you also create a tracking mechanism. For example, you may decide to track the number of times you get challenged in meetings. If you see that this metric is increasing over time, you can rest assured that you are building a more interactive environment. This type of deliberate tracking will help you with building discipline and creating personal accountability.

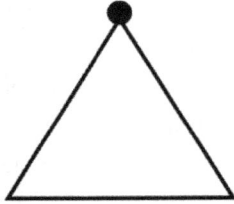

CHAPTER 1 - MOVING WITH PURPOSE

If you're not sure where you are going, you're liable to end up someplace else.

– Robert F. Mager

In the world of electronic communication, there is a metric called "signal-to-noise ratio." When data is communicated through wires over long distances, random noises creep in and corrupt it, sometimes making it indistinguishable from the noise. This is analogous to a conversation in a restaurant; if the environment is noisy, the "signal" from your friend across the table mixes with all the surrounding noise, making it difficult to understand what he or she is saying. In effect, the ratio of the signal to the noise is too low. The only way to make things better is to either increase the signal's strength or decrease the amount of noise.

When you are in the middle of a disruption or change event, the environment becomes noisy. Things evolve constantly, and information pours in from all directions. As you try to make sense of the situation, you must contend with not only all this external noise but also the inner noise created by your instincts, intuitions, and beliefs, all of which jostle for mind-space and push you in different directions.

This environmental noise exists not just for leaders but also for everyone else in the organization. Disruptions and change events bring uncertainty and stress, both of which induce strong feelings and reactions. Left to their own devices, people can formulate a worldview laced with cynicism and doomsday thinking. They can create their own inner noise that distracts, disheartens, and impedes progress. Things can grind to a halt exactly when they should be speeding up.

Here is the bottom line: change and disruption create noise, and organizations suffused with such noise cannot make meaningful progress. In such situations, it is critically important for leaders to create a strong signal that cuts through the noise. They must set a clear mission that focuses everyone on a common objective and inspires them to participate in the challenging journey to success.

1.1 SETTING A NORTH STAR

A North Star is a statement that tells an organization where they are going *right now*. It provides clarity of purpose by setting a specific and visible destination.

In the same way that the actual North Star[5] provided a steady signal to seafaring merchants during storms and blizzards, the enterprise North Star guides an organization's rank and file during times of change and disruption. It plays the role of an anchor amid the turbulence and unifies the organization around a common purpose.

The management team should set a North Star based on their interpretation of the organization's immediate priorities. It should have the following attributes:

1. *Meaningful*. The destination prescribed by the North Star should be meaningful and inspire everyone to contribute.

2. *Concise*. Ideally, it should fit in one or two sentences that capture the essence of what the organization wants to accomplish.

3. *Tangible*. People should be able to visualize what success will look like so that they can personally formulate actions to take them closer.

4. *Explainable*. Everyone should be able to understand and explain what the North Star is and why it was

---

[5] Polaris, also called the North Star or Pole Star, is the brightest star in the constellation of Ursa Minor.

set – this is critical for creating real buy-in.

5. *Unambiguous.* The North Star is a crucial tool for democratizing decision making in the organization. The destination it prescribes should not be subject to interpretation. Whenever there is confusion on which way to go, the North Star should be able to help break standoffs and set priorities.

A well-crafted North Star can go a long way in bringing clarity of purpose to an organization. It can even help large and complex organizations become agile by enabling different teams and siloes to move in lockstep towards a common destination.

This is a good time to also discuss what a North Star is not:

1. *It is not a vision statement,* which usually articulates a longer-term destination, that may or may not be reachable. The North Star is intentionally set for a shorter duration – its primary goal is to help an organization align around the next significant milestone.

2. *It is not a culture statement,* which usually describes aspirational values for the organization.

The North Star is a specific and touchable milestone, with a finite time horizon. It can be set at the team level or the enterprise level, depending on the size and scope of the situation.

Leaders must communicate the North Star often through various channels. They should refer to it publicly and regularly and make it part of their daily decision-making process. This type of reinforcement embeds the imperative into the organization's operating system.

An important feature of the North Star is that it sets a destination but does not prescribe a path to it. This approach allows everyone in the organization to personalize the mission and contribute to developing solutions. It also fosters agility when the ground realities evolve, and course corrections need to be made.

One of the best North Star statements I ever came across was the one used in the early stages of the Coronavirus pandemic. Even though the path forward was unclear, and confusion reigned supreme, the entire globe was able to get aligned around a short-term objective: "flatten the curve." In just three words, we had an inspirational, concise, actionable, explainable, and unambiguous goal that seven billion people could contribute to *in their own way*. It gave everyone some semblance of control over their destiny. It sparked many innovations from the grassroots that would not have been possible without a clear and unifying goal.

I would like you to take a timeout here and reflect on your organization's short-term mission. As you consider the following questions, bounce your ideas with others, and pressure test your assumptions.

1. Can you describe the top priority for your organization today?

2. Can you craft a North Star that clearly articulates this top priority? Does it have the five critical attributes we discussed?

3. How can you consistently communicate this priority and use it to guide your everyday work?

Timeout

Welcome back. I hope that was a thought-provoking exercise. Establishing a North Star is a *critical* first step for shepherding an organization through disruption or crisis, or for that matter, any other change initiative. It is a hygiene issue that *must* be taken care of before you jump into actual problem-solving.

That said, there is another essential prerequisite for success that you must put in place proactively and manage actively. That prerequisite is aligning your leadership and peers towards your North Star.

1.2 ALIGNING UP THE LEADERSHIP CHAIN

The biggest distractions during a disruption sometimes come from leaders above you, especially if they are under pressure from their own customers and shareholders. This can make them impatient, want frequent updates, and push new ideas in your direction on an almost daily basis.

The last thing you want during a crisis is a bunch of distractions. As you start to focus your team on your North Star, you must ensure that the leadership layers above you are also aligned with your priorities. Your work will not stop after this first step – you will need to actively manage expectations and keep everyone focused on the top few things that move the needle. If you do not do this, you will find yourself continually changing direction and making little progress.

I recall an incident from my time in India when I was presenting my organization's strategy to the regional leadership team. There were many senior people in the room that day, and each one seemed to want something different. I was under a lot of pressure to say yes to everyone. I stood my ground, however, and forced the group to work together and make some hard choices. We had a robust discussion, and to everyone's credit, we managed to get aligned on the most critical priorities by the end of the meeting.

After that, whenever a new idea or suggestion was made, we judged it on its merits, compared it with the baseline plan, and came to a collective decision whether to stay the course or pivot. This deliberate approach forced everyone to take responsibility for changes and their resulting impact on business outcomes. It also prevented frequent course corrections and brought stability to the working team.

I would now like you to take a short timeout and consider the following questions. Take your time and answer the questions honestly – these are foundational elements of leading through change, and shortcuts won't get you anywhere.

1. Is your organization operating with a clear set of priorities that have been aligned with your leadership chain? Do you feel like you have the freedom to work autonomously without second-guessing from your leaders?

2. If you answered yes to the above questions, what enabled you to achieve this type of healthy alignment? How are you actively managing it? Is there anything you could do better?

3. If you answered no, what do you think contributed to the lack of alignment? What can you do to fix it?

Timeout

Welcome back. I hope you found the exercise useful and came up with ways to strengthen *vertical* alignment across your leadership chain. Once you have achieved this, you will need to turn your focus immediately towards *horizontal* alignment with your peers and stakeholders. This is another critical prerequisite for success that, if not appropriately managed, can actively work to undermine your efforts.

1.3 ELIMINATING SILOS

It was late in the evening, and I was dialed into a teleconference with senior leaders from across the globe. I was walking everyone through some recent bad news on a project when one of my colleagues interjected and started speaking. It was not just any colleague; he was someone I worked with closely. To my dismay, he proceeded to contradict several things I had just said, putting me in a very awkward position. *What was he doing? I thought we were sitting on the same side of the table!*

My first instinct was to blame my colleague personally. I realized after some reflection, however, that the real underlying reason for his behavior was misaligned objectives. He was one of my many stakeholders, all of whom had different metrics for success. He was simply looking at things from his point of view and trying to ensure success for his team.

Through this painful experience, I learned that when people in an organization have different criteria for success and remuneration, they can end up working at cross purposes with each other. People who are nice and genial in social settings can become combative and uncooperative in professional ones as they try to maximize their own metrics.

This kind of behavior should not surprise us. Tribalism has existed for as long as humans have walked the earth, with people protecting their interests and watching out for their own. That said, if you are a leader trying to shepherd your organization through change, this is the last thing you want from your team.

Many change initiatives fail because of a lack of alignment. A recent survey[6] of over two hundred corporate leaders found that the top obstacle for innovation is "politics / turf wars / no alignment." This type of behavior pits team against team, each protecting their silo while actively competing for resources. It creates heartburn and erodes trust.

The most problematic misalignments tend to be financial. Let me illustrate with an example. Imagine a scenario where the Engineering department of a company proposes a new design for their product that will slightly increase the manufacturing cost but will also improve its quality and reduce its maintenance cost. In effect, this idea would reduce the overall cost to the company while improving its brand reputation – this should be a no-brainer, right? One would think so. However, if the incentives for the manufacturing

---

[6] The Biggest Obstacles to Innovation in Large Companies, Scott Kirsner, Harvard Business Review, July 30, 2018

organization are based on factory profits, its leaders will not buy into the proposal because the increased manufacturing cost will impact their year-end bonus. Hence, instead of cooperating on what is a fundamentally good idea, they will drag their feet, and prevent the idea from crossing the finish line.

Is the above example not realistic? Surely, people understand the importance of teamwork, especially in times of crisis? Unfortunately, the answer is no. Even on critical initiatives that everyone agrees are important, you will see little forward movement if you do not align the participants' financial incentives. Every person wants to know "what's in it for me?" before they can decide if they want to get on board.

Aligning metrics and incentives is the job of leaders at the top. They are the ones who can see the full picture and decide where cooperation is essential.

If you are a leader in the C-suite, it is *your* job to get a full appreciation of what is needed to achieve success and then work with your peers to set the right incentive structure. If you are a leader below the C-suite, your job is to ensure that all the inter-dependencies for success are visible to the people above you so they can do their jobs properly.

Incentives can be structured in different ways –

- centralized, where the metrics and bonuses are set based on the company achieving its objectives,

- decentralized, where the metrics and bonuses

are set based on the specific team achieving its objectives, and

- hybrid, where the metrics and bonuses are based on a weighted combination of the two.

When working on an initiative where all functions must pull together in the same direction, it is best to set centralized incentives that reward collective success over individual brilliance. This approach encourages everyone to sit on the same side of the table and actively help each other succeed.

On the other hand, if the company has separate teams and divisions that are expected to operate independently and be entrepreneurial, decentralized objectives might work better.

Even after appropriate incentives have been designed, it can take a lot of effort to drive the right behavior, especially if the various teams are led by opinionated and powerful people who like to flex their muscles in public. *Leaders must call out bad behavior when they see it*. They must also visibly reward good behavior and make it clear to the broader organization that these are the actions they expect everyone to model and emulate.

Sometimes you may find a situation that is just not fixable, for instance, when people don't change or carry way too much baggage from the past. In such cases, it might be better to reassign these people and bring in new leaders. Installing new faces can sometimes go a long way in resetting broken relationships and creating a fresh start.

Here is the bottom line: Cross-functional alignment is a critical prerequisite for moving forward with purpose. It is in your best interest to build a strong and inclusive coalition with your stakeholders and work with them to achieve collective success.

I would like you to stop here and consider the following questions. Please keep an open mind as you answer them – this is an emotional topic that can easily get influenced by past bad experiences.

1. Identify the key stakeholders and departments whose cooperation is essential to your success. Are you experiencing problems with any of them? If yes, how openly visible are these problems?

2. Can any of the problems be traced to misaligned incentives? What can you do to fix them?

3. Have you ever been guilty of assuming the worst about one or more of your peers even though they may have been merely behaving in a certain way because of their incentive structure? If that relationship is still alive, how can you "reset" it and make it healthier?

4. Do you meet regularly with your key stakeholders and ensure alignment of priorities? If not, can you set up such a process?

Timeout

Welcome back. I hope you were able to identify some concrete actions to foster better alignment and teamwork with your stakeholders. It will be critical to your future success.

CHAPTER SUMMARY

In this chapter, we discussed the importance of creating a clear sense of purpose and direction for your organization during times of change and disruption. Setting clear expectations and managing organizational relationships are the critical first steps of Inpowering Leadership. They set the team up for success by fostering trust and focusing everyone on the most critical priorities.

We discussed two specific steps: 1) crafting a clear and actionable North Star and 2) aligning senior leaders and stakeholders around it. These steps will help you cut through the noise and confusion that usually reign during times of disruption and enable everyone in your organization to visualize and align around a shared, tangible destination.

I cannot emphasize enough the importance of getting the above steps right. During my years as a leader, whenever I was able to align my superiors, peers, and team-mates around a set of "vital few" priorities, we made meaningful progress, and the outcomes were good. When I was unable to build this type of consensus, however, we ended up with a lot of second-guessing, a palpable lack of progress, and a drop in organizational morale.

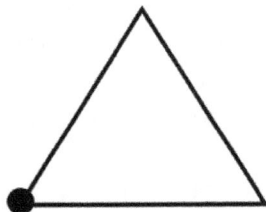

CHAPTER 2 - MOVING WITH SPEED

Leaders don't create followers. They create more leaders.

– Tom Peters

Early in my career, I was nominated to attend a two-week executive development program at a prestigious business school. I was part of a select group of mid-level managers who had been identified as having the potential to be the next senior leaders at my company.

The program was like a mini-MBA. The sessions were run by highly knowledgeable and engaging faculty members who used the case study approach to make us think deeply about various aspects of running a business.

Within the first couple of days of the program, I noticed a curious phenomenon. At the end of every session, some of my classmates immediately headed for the exits, switched on their phones, and started calling people. I found this curious and asked one of them what was going on. His response was surprising. He told me that he had to call his team every few hours because he could not trust them to keep things running smoothly while he was away. He made light of the situation, perhaps because of the expression on my face, but his attitude made it quite clear that he did not trust his second line to step up during his absence.

Does this sound at all familiar to you? Please take a short timeout to consider the following questions.

1. Have you ever worked for someone who constantly followed up and micro-managed you? How did it make you feel, and how effectively were you able to perform your job?

2. How would you describe your own management style when it comes to trust and empowerment? Do you find it difficult to delegate work to others? Do you tend to follow up, even while away on vacation? (Hint: ask your family – they will give you an honest answer.)

Timeout

Welcome back. I hope you discovered some things about yourself as you answered these questions. Your observations will serve as a good foundation for the coming sections.

2.1 HOW TO UNLEASH INNER POWER

A few years ago, I read a book called "Dance with Chance." The book's premise was that most people tend to overestimate their ability to influence the world around them. They try to control what cannot be controlled and predict what cannot be predicted, thus creating mental anguish and dissatisfying outcomes.

The book provided a lot of examples ranging from investing in the stock market to the accuracy of medical science. My main takeaway was this: in an uncertain world with many moving parts, it is hard to predict and control outcomes. A simpler and perhaps better approach is to *do the right things and let the outcomes follow*.

Many people have a management style where they try to control outcomes by trying to control the people who deliver those outcomes. This approach is more common than we might think. Most managers get into positions of responsibility because they have shown in previous assignments that they can get things done. They are usually hardworking, attentive to detail, and results oriented. When such high achievers are put into management roles, they can sometimes treat the people reporting to them as just another set of tools to meet their milestones and objectives.

Humans are, unfortunately (or fortunately!) quite different from machines and tools. We are complex creatures capable of generating a broad spectrum of outputs depending on our level of motivation and skills. Although some of us are happy to follow instructions and do exactly as we are told, others can do much more if they are empowered and let loose on problems.

In today's fast-moving world, leaders who treat their staff as robots and feed them piecemeal instructions are doing it all wrong. This approach simply increases their own workload because they must now not only manage their own tasks but also (micro) manage the work being done by everyone else. Imagine if they could instead get their people to organically create value and content – they could be so much more effective and efficient!

Over my career, I had the pleasure of working with all sorts of leaders. The ones I liked most were those who valued what I brought to the table. They explained what they were trying to achieve, worked with me to define what part I could play, and then let me figure out the details. I was not only responsible for developing solutions but also accountable for achieving the outcomes. That was true empowerment! It got my creative juices flowing and instilled a strong sense of purpose. In the end, what I delivered was probably much better than what my boss could have envisaged.

I also had the chance to work with a couple of leaders who could not trust me to get the job done. They second-guessed my actions, made changes after a lot of work had already been done, and always tried to have the last word. Unfortunately, their inability to "let go" prevented them from fully leveraging my skills and capabilities. Also, their lack of trust changed my mindset from that of a leader to that of a manager whose primary focus was to deliver what was promised – nothing more, nothing less.

Lastly, I got to work with some leaders who tried to straddle the line. They started by micro-managing me and slowly increased my autonomy as I proved myself. Although this seemed like a sensible approach, I soon realized that it was not efficient. Why did I have to start from scratch every time I had a new boss? How could this possibly motivate me or bring the best out of me? Would it not be better to start from a position of trust and give me a chance to show what I was capable of?

As I worked with various leaders, I observed how their operating style impacted my colleagues and me. This is what I found: the quality and quantity of our output were directly correlated with the amount of empowerment and autonomy we were given. *The leaders who truly ignited our core were the ones who gave us full ownership of significant activities and the freedom to develop solutions.* These Inpowering Leaders started from a position of trust and were willing to take on the risk that came with it. In essence, these leaders were willing to *dance with chance.*

Please stop here and take a timeout to reflect on your management style. As you think about the below questions, put yourself in the shoes of your direct reports, and imagine what life looks like from their perspective.

1. Of the three management styles I just described, which one best describes you? Can you think about why you operate in this way? Did some of your formative experiences influence your appetite for trust and delegation?

2. Where on this empowerment spectrum would you like to sit going forward? How can you get there?

Timeout

Welcome back. So far, we have discussed how things look from the employee's perspective when leaders empower and trust them. Let us now jump into the benefits of empowerment from the leader's perspective – why they should do it and what they can gain from it.

2.2 BUILDING A BENCH

In the early 2000s, I took on a role at one of my company's divisions as their global expert in acoustics. I spent the next few years traveling to various countries, helping teams develop quieter products.

This was an exciting phase of my career. I was solving complex real-world problems, and my time was always in high demand. I was also constantly busy, working long hours, and spending less time with my family. These experiences brought me to the following realizations:

- Being a go-to expert made me feel great, but it was also highly draining and gave me little time to think beyond day-to-day challenges.

- As I got busier, I was becoming a bottleneck. If I taught more people to do what I did, I could drive greater velocity and efficiency at an organizational scale.

I embarked on an aggressive journey of teaching. I used the proverbial 80/20 rule, where I taught fellow engineers how to do 80% of my work so I could focus on the most complex 20%. I ran seminars and hands-on workshops across the globe with a focus on basic problem-solving and design skills.

In a few years, I started to see measurable outcomes. The knowledge I imparted spread organically through the organization. Engineers were now able to take direct control of many of their issues without my help.

Many years later, I was in a meeting with an engineer who showed me how he had diagnosed a complex mechanical issue. As he walked me through his analysis, I recognized some of the charts and plots; they were based on the very same methods I had taught many years earlier. There were some differences, however. The engineer had extended my methods in novel ways and was deriving insights that I had not imagined were possible. His work was a beautiful example of organic growth through autonomy.

The above experience, along with many other similar ones, taught me in a very tangible way what could be achieved when you freely share knowledge and empower others. Every time I did this, I was designing myself out of a job. In parallel, however, I was also amplifying my impact to the organization by creating a larger force of people who could autonomously solve problems. There were three significant effects:

- *Increased velocity* – by training others and building a bench, I eliminated a big bottleneck – myself – from the problem-solving process.

- *Increased bandwidth* – because others were now performing many of my tasks, I had more time to think about strategy and growth, a critical part of my role as a leader.

- *Increased freedom* – over time, I made it possible for me to move on and explore new assignments without worrying that things would break after my departure.

Building a bench can help an organization move with greater speed during times of disruption. But it is not easy to pull off. Empowering others can be difficult for some people because it fundamentally removes them from the day-to-day information loop. They love being at the center of the action, doling out sage advice that everyone treats like gold. Unfortunately, being at the center of everything is also inherently limiting and exhausting. Not only does it slow you down, it also leads to burnout.

If you want to grow your impact and help your organization move faster, you will need to *let go* and actively empower others. Operating this way will enable you to multiply your contributions and deliver outcomes larger than what you could accomplish as an individual. It will create bandwidth for you to think strategically and explore new opportunities. And finally, it will allow you to cut the cord and move on to new things. In short, *empowering others will set you free.*

I recall a television advertisement for a motorcycle from my teenage years in India. The tagline was – "fill it, shut it, forget it" – which implied that you could fill the tank with gas and then forget about it because the high fuel efficiency of the bike would keep it running for days[7]. I think of empowerment similarly. The most valuable players in my team have always been the ones who could take problems and fully own them. I could

---

[7] Hero Honda was a motorcycle with a four-stroke engine that changed the game on fuel efficiency

"forget it" after I had delegated my tasks to them. If they needed anything, they would come and find me. If I heard nothing from them, it meant that they were on top of things and would likely show up to our next checkpoint, having met all their milestones.

This is an excellent place to stop, reflect, and do some self-calibration. Please be honest as you answer the following questions – that is the only way to come up with meaningful actions.

1. How do you rate yourself when it comes to knowledge sharing? How actively have you worked to grow your people such that they are less dependent on you?

2. If you have held back on sharing your knowledge, what are your reasons? Have there been past bad experiences that are driving this behavior? Do you think that behaving this way might be limiting your growth opportunities?

3. Who are the "empower and forget-it" players in your organization? How are you investing in them? Please develop a few actions that you can put into play in the coming days.

Timeout

Welcome back. I hope you found that exercise somewhat uncomfortable. The idea of freely teaching others to take your job can be difficult to internalize. That said, it is a highly effective way to multiply your contributions to the enterprise and move it forward with speed.

2.3 SHARING THE LIMELIGHT

During my expatriate in India, I took three annual vacations with my family. All of them were timed with my children's school vacations.

One year, I was getting ready to head out for our spring break vacation when I got a note from our company's president. He was planning to visit our facility during the week that I would be away. We were in the middle of some critical projects and a visit by such a senior leader created a strong impulse to try and be there. I decided, however, to proceed with my vacation.

For the previous two years, I had worked hard to build a solid second-line who fully understood what we were doing, why we were doing it, and how we were going about it. I felt confident that my deputies would do a great job in my absence. So, without thinking too hard, I sent a note to the president welcoming him to our facility. I told him that, unfortunately, I would be on vacation, but my team would take care of him and ensure that all his questions were answered. He replied that this was perfectly fine and wished my family a fun and safe outing.

This type of situation has occurred many times during my career. I have never thought twice about leaning on my team. And every time, I have been pleasantly surprised by how well things have gone in my absence.

Of course, I would never do this type of thing without building a capable second line and ensuring that they are adequately prepared. But cutting the cord and letting others step up has been one of my best ways of growing the next generation of leaders.

Why do I so strongly believe in this approach? Simply because I have been the beneficiary of the same approach on many occasions.

During the early part of my career, I was fortunate to work with leaders who genuinely believed in me and did not hesitate to let me enjoy the limelight. They steadily upped the ante by delegating larger and larger tasks and initiatives, along with their complete and visible backing. They let me represent them during important meetings and presentations and allowed me to command the agenda without their lingering shadow.

Every time this happened, I experienced the nervous energy and trepidation that comes from new and unfamiliar situations. But this only pushed me to prepare hard and rise to the occasion. And with every experience, I grew my skills and expertise.

One of my mentors used to say, "none of us were ready for the next job we were thrust into." What he meant was that none of us grew professionally because we were put into roles that we could already do; *we grew because we were entrusted with next-level roles that our leaders thought that we could do*. For me, this is the essence of how you develop the next generation of leaders and talent.

Unfortunately, I have also seen the opposite play out. Some leaders refuse to promote people until they are already exhibiting all the skills required at the next level. This creates a farcical game where a carrot is dangled just a little ahead, and the discussion focuses on the 10% of skills that you are yet to demonstrate, rather than the 90% you already have. This is an approach that deflates rather than inspires. It betrays a lack of trust and is antithetical to growth.

I have experienced both approaches – being entrusted with a stretch assignment versus being asked first to prove that I could do the job. There is no comparison. I experienced a massive increase in motivation when leaders took a chance and placed their trust in me.

When I started managing others, I decided to embrace the same approach. If I believed that people in my team were capable *and* desirous of taking on more, I went ahead and gave them more responsibility and, when appropriate, pushed for their promotion. I created opportunities for them to represent me in strategic discussions and stepped away from the limelight when possible.

The outcomes were generally good and sometimes spectacular. I saw many talented people bloom and come into their own when given opportunities to flex and grow. Watching them transform was among the most satisfying experiences of my career. It allowed me to leave behind a legacy that would persist well after I had moved on.

I would like you to stop here and indulge in some introspection. The following questions will help calibrate your willingness to step away from the action and delegate. Please answer them with honesty and use them as a means to stretch your thinking.

1. How comfortable are you with the idea of your subordinates making a presentation to your superiors without you being present? If you are uncomfortable with this idea, why?

2. Can you recall any incidents where your leaders empowered you to represent them in important meetings or discussions? If yes, how did that feel, and what did it do for your professional growth?

3. Can you come up with some ways to let your deputies swim in deeper waters without you standing by as a lifeguard?

Timeout

Welcome back. I hope you came up with some concrete ways to let your second line experience what it is like to be in your shoes. Depending on your current operating style, this may or may not be easy for you. I encourage you to find ways to get there – you might be pleasantly surprised by the outcomes.

We are not done. I would like you to think a little more about this topic. In the next set of questions, I would like you to think about your team's superstars and what you are doing to nurture and grow them.

1. Are there people in your team who you sincerely admire and believe could exceed your achievements given the right opportunities? What are you doing to help them achieve their full potential?

2. How do you feel about helping people who could eventually replace you or even become your superiors? Are you comfortable with imagining such scenarios? Why or why not?

Timeout

Welcome back. I hope you spent some time exploring these questions. They get to the core of what empowerment and delegation are all about – *creating the next generation of leaders who can amplify your impact and help you implement your vision*. To accomplish this, you must be ready to let others own parts of what you do and sometimes do them better than you.

You cannot get there by half measures; these techniques are only effective when the immersion is total. If you are not comfortable with this, you may want to take a step back and rethink your role as a leader.

When you empower someone to represent you, it is a covenant built on trust. You are trusting your delegate to do a job on your behalf. You expect it to be done at a level of quality that you are proud of, with little intervention from you. That can only happen when both sides of the transaction trust each other to hold their end of the bargain.

But what if this arrangement does not work? What if your delegate performs poorly or misuses their empowered status? Is there a way you can manage this?

2.4 BUILDING AN ACCOUNTABLE TEAM

When I first became a manager, I decided that the only way to treat my team was to empower everyone and make them fully accountable for outcomes. I learned over time, however, that not everyone reacted to empowerment the same way I did. Instead, they roughly fell into one of four buckets.

ACCOUNTABILITY	**II** Tell me what you want I will find you if I need help	**I** Let me figure things out I will find you if I need help
	IV Tell me what you want Check in on me regularly	**III** Let me figure things out Check in on me regularly

EMPOWERMENT AND AUTONOMY

Group I: These were highly motivated individuals who loved autonomy, could independently solve problems, and could be relied upon to deliver without much following up. They were the top players in my team and the go-to people for new and complex challenges. I actively invested in their growth and nurtured them for leadership assignments.

Group II: These were people who liked clear instructions and always delivered with accuracy and precision. They were the mainstay of the organization – hardworking, skilled, focused, and reliable. I did everything I could to grow their skillsets and keep them motivated.

Group III: These were people who demanded autonomy but were easily distracted and could not deliver without constant supervision. They required high maintenance and drained me mentally as well as physically with little to show for it. I moved them out of my organization as fast as I could[8].

Group IV: These were people who needed a lot of handholding. Many of them were new hires, fresh out of school, who simply needed some time to learn the ropes and become productive. Others were bad hiring decisions. They were given a reasonable amount of time to move into Group I or II. If they could not make it, they were let go.

It took me a few years as a manager to figure all this out. I learned that my time was best spent on Group I and II – *these were the people who I could trust to amplify my impact*. I gave them as much responsibility as they could handle and then stepped aside. I set up regular checkpoints to coach them and remove roadblocks.

When a new person joined my team, I tried to err on the side of trust rather than caution. I gave them ownership of some important deliverables and observed how they handled the responsibility. If they did well and asked for more, I upped the ante and gave them as much as they could handle. If they were unable to keep up, I backed off. After a few cycles trial and error, we usually settled into a rhythm and took things from there.

My experiences taught me that empowerment and accountability are two sides of the same coin. You cannot have one without the other. When they do come

---

[8] If they had a niche skill that I could not replace easily, I immediately started working on a backup plan so that I could remove my dependence on them at the earliest.

together, however, you get to witness a magical phenomenon where *the leader and the delegate operate in lockstep, each inpowering the other* to ever greater heights.

This is an excellent place to stop and take a timeout. As you answer the following questions, I would like you to think about the people in your team and how you can flex the amount you empower each one.

1. Do you have a good sense of who the Group I, II, III, and IV players are in your team?

2. Who are the people you spend the most time with? Do you think you might need to change this up?

3. Are you giving stretch assignments to the people in Group I? How are you setting up accountability mechanisms that keep you in the loop without stifling autonomy and speed?

4. Do you have any Group III players? Are they adding enough value to be worth keeping in your team? What is your plan for them?

Timeout

Welcome back. So far, in this chapter, we have described the key benefits of empowerment and walked through some practical steps to implement it. Next, we will discuss how you can further accelerate this culture within your organization and get more significant benefits in return.

2.5 MOVING TO A CULTURE OF YES

The following quote is attributed to Warren Buffett: "Very successful people say no to almost everything." The premise is that leaders are laser-focused on what is essential and have the strength to say no to everything else.

Although I cannot disagree with the premise, I am not too fond of how it is worded. If you have to say no to *almost everything* that comes your way, it means that either you are getting a lot of unreasonable requests or you are constantly second-guessing your team. This type of behavior is unhealthy, inefficient, and erodes trust.

A much better way to operate would be to empower your team with not only the responsibility to deliver outcomes but also the contextual information they need to be successful. If everyone clearly understands the organization's mission and the parameters within which they must operate, then the requests that they make of their leaders will likely be well thought out and result in a yes.

Moving to a culture of yes is a powerful way to build trust and momentum in an organization. It is not easy, mind you – it takes a lot of effort, especially upfront. Everyone in the team must be brought to the same level of understanding as the leader, and new information must be flowed down in a timely manner. Everyone must know the prevailing priorities, constraints, and idiosyncrasies that could impact decision making.

For example, the company may be in a short-term cash crunch, which means requests for capital authorizations will likely be denied unless critical. If the people on the team know this, they will adjust their expectations and only ask for mission critical things.

If you say yes more often, it will have two positive side effects. First, it will free up your time because you will be merely taking a cursory glance at requests that easily pass muster. Second, every time you say yes, your team will feel validated and trusted. They will experience a sense of autonomy (albeit within constraints) and continue to move forward with purpose.

On the flip side, saying no a lot, even for justifiable reasons, will annihilate any desire within your team to take the initiative. If anything, you might be better off doing the opposite and sometimes saying yes even when you are not 100% sure. It will give your team the chance to take some risks and learn from the outcomes.

It is hard to overstate the efficiencies that can be created by moving to a culture of yes. I have personally seen the minutiae that can sometimes submerge leaders and make them work long hours. I once got an email during the weekend because an approval request from one of my team members had gotten bumped up to my boss. The request was to upgrade his cell phone plan because he was traveling out of the country on vacation. This request required two levels of approval and had hence gone to my superior, who was now asking for justification. I replied with the rationale for the request, and it was promptly approved. But think about what had just happened. Two senior executives had spent precious time during the weekend approving something that would cost their firm almost nothing. We were only doing our jobs, but why did we even have a two-level approval for this? And what did every such request do to the trust between us and our subordinates?

Inpowering Leaders understand the importance of empowering their people and eliminating approval steps and layers. They increase velocity by building a culture of yes and delegating as much as possible to the lower levels of their organization.

This is a good time for reflection. Let's take a moment to calibrate how well your organization is in sync with your expectations. I recommend you talk with your team as part of this exercise.

1. Think back to your last few months at work. Have you been saying no to a lot of things? If so, what is driving this?

2. Can you think of some instances where you said no but could have said yes without losing too much sleep over it?

3. Have you done a solid job of communicating priorities and setting expectations with your team? Do you think they clearly understand the prevailing business pressures and constraints?

4. What does the financial approval process look like in your organization? Are there opportunities to delegate more things to lower levels?

5. What else can you do to give your team more autonomy?

Timeout

Welcome back. I hope you generated some actions to move your operating paradigm to yes. This will not just increase speed and efficiency, but also improve morale and work satisfaction for your team. Try it. You will not be disappointed.

Now that you have effectively empowered your second line, it is time for you to go deeper you're your organization, all the way down to the grassroots. It is time to start operating bottoms-up.

2.6 OPERATING BOTTOMS-UP

At the start of one of my assignments, I was quickly inundated with large quantities of email. As the new guy, I was happy to see this rapid engagement from my team and their desire to get me up to speed. I soon realized, however, that a lot of the emails were requests for some sort of review or approval.

As the leader, I expected to be in the approval chain for things like purchase requests and capital. I was, however, also getting requests to review deliverables and action items on projects and initiatives. Since these projects had designated leaders, I did not understand why I was in the approval loop for anything.

I talked with some of my peers and learned that the organization had developed a culture where all important decisions were routed upwards for approval. This system ensured that nothing of significance could go forward without the full management chain's blessing. I was just the logical endpoint in this process.

This situation is not uncommon. It is present in organizations where the management has a "top-down" style of operation. In such environments, leaders enjoy a high level of discretion and get to approve or veto all decisions. Unfortunately, this can result in micro-management and regular second-guessing of calls taken by subordinates. When this happens regularly, the team defaults to getting all decisions reviewed and ratified by their superiors. That is the only way they can cover their backs and prevent surprises down the line.

Top-down management is inherently slow because every decision is bottlenecked and paced by the multiple layers of decision-makers. It is a terrible way to operate in today's fast-changing world when execution speed is critical to your success. What you want instead is an autonomous and nimble organization that can move forward without constant adult supervision.

To build such an organization, you must cut the red tape. You must equip your people with all the information and tools they need to get the job done. You must encourage them to be proactive and assure them that you will have their back if things go wrong. You must create an environment of autonomy and accountability *all the way to the bottom* where *every person* in the organization knows what is expected of them and has the authority to execute within his or her domain of expertise. In short, *you must operate bottoms-up*.

To operate bottoms-up, you will have to not only empower your direct reports but also get them to do the same with their teams, and so on. You will need to show through your actions that some level of risk-taking is not just okay but encouraged. Some ways to do this include providing discretionary budgets to experiment with new ideas, recognizing entrepreneurial behavior, and rewarding managers who visibly foster this mindset in their teams.

Once you have established a bottoms-up culture, the next issue you must tackle is information flow. Bottoms-up organizations are fast-moving by design. Once people understand what is expected of them, they develop their plans and get going. Unfortunately, in today's dynamic world, the facts on the ground can change quite quickly. A solid plan from yesterday can become outdated or irrelevant tomorrow because of a sudden change in the business or competitive environment. If the people in the organization are not kept in the loop, they may continue expending valuable cash and resources on activities that no longer make sense.

To avoid waste, leaders must ensure that information moves quickly across the organization. The latest market developments and resulting course corrections should be communicated as soon as possible so that everyone can make necessary adjustments to their plans and keep moving forward in lockstep.

Many organizations do not get this right. Sometimes, management holds cards close to their chest, either because they want to wait till things are finalized or because they think their organization cannot handle the truth. Unfortunately, information vacuums are not desirable even in the best of times. They can be truly harmful during crises.

It is a bad idea for leaders to act like everything is fine when things are getting visibly difficult. People can resort to rumormongering and get distracted from the mission. It is better that leaders honestly acknowledge the situation, empathetically listen to their peoples' concerns, and include them in the journey to develop solutions. They should ensure that everyone is current on developments and operating off the same set of information. They can achieve this through regular all-hands meetings as well as just-in-time updates via online channels.

Here is the bottom line: *Information is empowering.* It provides context and decentralizes decision making. When communicated promptly, it results in a highly responsive organization that works on the most critical and value-adding activities. It enables autonomy at the grassroots and allows everyone to move forward with speed.

I would like you to hit pause and reflect on ways to make your organization operate bottom-up. As you answer the following questions, think about how you can improve information flow and foster decision-making at your organization's lowest levels.

1. Do you find that a lot of decisions and priority calls get delegated upward to you? If yes, what could you do to pull yourself out of the approval loop and drive more autonomy at your organization's lower levels?

2. How quickly does information flow in your organization today? Do you use multiple mechanisms for communicating news and recent business developments?

3. How well informed are your people? If you walked around your workplace and talked with the people on your team, would they have a good pulse for what is happening at the company level?

4. How engaged and invested are your people in your organization's journey? Can they explain the organizational priorities and how their work contributes to the big picture?

5. How entrepreneurial is the culture in your organization? What can you do to encourage a stronger orientation towards action? Can you find ways to incentivize and recognize such behaviors?

⏳ **Timeout**

Welcome back. I hope you thought of some good ways to drive empowerment and autonomy at all levels of your organization. It is not an easy thing to pull off. It requires a coordinated and sustained effort by all levels of management. But when it does happen, you end up with a focused, coordinated, and fast-moving organization.

CHAPTER SUMMARY

In this chapter, we discussed how to increase organizational speed by decentralizing decision-making and empowering everyone to take direct action.

We started with techniques for developing a reliable second line of leaders who own significant parts of your responsibilities and amplify your impact on the enterprise. We talked about the importance of trust and how it impacts your willingness to delegate. We also discussed the relationship between trust and accountability and the need to build a team that delivers consistently on its commitments.

With the above foundation in place, we explored ways to push the culture of empowerment deeper into your organization. We talked about moving to a "culture of yes," by removing approval layers for less consequential decisions. We also discussed the concept of operating bottoms-up, where everyone in the organization is encouraged to interpret the mission and contribute in their own way.

All the above techniques provide a solid recipe to increase the speed and efficiency of your enterprise. And as you may have noticed, all of them have a common underlying requirement: *trust*.

Empowerment is an inherently risky undertaking. It requires you to cut the cord and let others take control of your responsibilities. None of this is possible without trust.

There is a story from IBM about a young executive who made some bad decisions that cost the company over a million dollars. He was summoned to the CEO's office, where he fully expected to be fired. After explaining the details of the deal and all the mistakes he had made, the salesman handed the CEO a letter of resignation. The CEO supposedly handed back the envelope saying: "why would I fire you when I have just invested a million dollars in your education?"

This story provides the essence of what it means to empower others. It requires accepting that risks will be taken, and mistakes will be made. That said, you can manage some of the risks by providing your people with the information and resources they need to succeed. If you do this, the outcomes should be statistically positive.

Inpowering Leaders start from a position of trust. They use empowerment as a means to unleash their team's inner talent and build an autonomous army of lieutenants. Operating this way enables them to make contributions that far exceed what they could have individually imagined or delivered. As this culture of empowerment flows lower and lower into their organization, the compounding effects only increase.

General George S. Patton summed it up quite well: "Don't tell people how to do things. Tell them what to do and let them surprise you with their results."

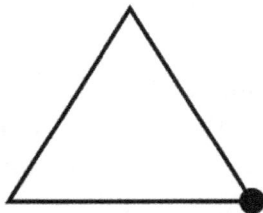

CHAPTER 3 - MOVING WITH ACCURACY

It doesn't make sense to hire smart people and
tell them what to do; we hire smart people so
they can tell us what to do.

– Steve Jobs

It was a beautiful spring morning. I was with a group of senior executives who had assembled for a day of team-building exercises. We did not know what to expect. All we knew was that we had to wear comfortable clothes and be ready for some physical activities.

Once I arrived, I was assigned to a team with four other people I had never interacted with before. For the next few hours, we participated in a series of physical and mental challenges that pushed us to our limits. Although the entire day was highly memorable, two specific sessions stayed with me over the years. They taught me a lot about myself and the people I work with every day.

The first was a physical challenge which, on its face, seemed impossible. We were given a task, along with some rules and constraints, and told to get it done within a specified amount of time.

The task looked absurd every way we looked at it. I searched the faces of my teammates, but no one seemed to have answers.

We started bouncing some ideas. At first, the discussion felt farcical. We were like blind people throwing darts at a board, hoping one would land near the target. But as we kept talking, some promising ideas started to emerge. Eventually we got to a plan – a difficult but seemingly workable one.

We were up against the clock, so we began to hustle. We executed each step of our strategy and adjusted it as unanticipated problems emerged. Curiously, things became easier as we made progress. And then the adrenaline kicked in! We executed one step after another, and before we knew it, the task was complete, well before the clock ran out.

It was unbelievable! What had seemed impossible at first had somehow become possible. Was it merely because of solid teamwork, or had there been more to it?

We moved on to the second exercise which was a maze. Getting through it required good problem-solving skills and a high level of physical cooperation. We took one step at a time and focused on solving each challenge as it presented itself. We made quick progress and soon found ourselves at the finish line with half of the allotted time remaining.

One by one, my teammates crossed over and exchanged high-fives. Then it was my turn, and I decided to jump across the finish line with a big flourish. As I leaped into the air, I saw a look of dismay cross over the faces of my teammates. In my excitement, I had broken one of the rules of the game, which was to always have one foot on the ground. Our coach stepped in and advised us that because of this one mistake, We would have to start over!

This was a very painful moment that would have broken most teams. What happened in our case, however, was completely different. Instead of pointing fingers, my teammates noticed the crestfallen look on my face and empathized with how terrible I must be feeling. One of them put their arm around me and said: "It's okay; we still have time to go back to the start line and do it again." I looked around and got approving nods from everyone. And that was all it took to lift me out of the depths of disappointment and back into competitive mode.

We raced back to the starting point and began moving with deliberate urgency. Since we were navigating the maze a second time, we knew exactly what we had to do at each step – this was now all about execution. Fast forward to the ending – we made it across the entire maze again, with time to spare. And this time, as we celebrated, I could sense that the five of us had forged a special kind of relationship.

Later that evening, I marveled at how our team had completed all the day's challenges, something that few other teams had managed to do. What had enabled us to achieve this type of consistent success? To me, it primarily boiled down to two things.

The first was *humility*. All of us were humble enough to accept that we did not have all the answers. Bear in mind that each of us was a senior leader at the company. We were used to taking charge of situations and felt some level of pressure to differentiate ourselves from our peers. That said, when thrust into an uncertain high-pressure environment, we automatically pivoted into a mode of collaboration. I must admit that it was hard for me to overrule my instincts and embrace ideas proposed by others. But even so, I chose to do it, and so did everyone else.

The second thing that enabled our success was *empathy*. I had somehow been teamed up with four of the kindest individuals I ever met. Even under pressure, when things went wrong, they were willing to give each other the benefit of the doubt. This fostered trust, which in turn helped five very different people put their minds together and work their way out of numerous tricky situations.

Whenever I think about that day, my brain starts channeling Maximus and his band of warriors in the Gladiator arena. Maximus was a famous general who had won many battles. He was used to leading from the front and had seen every possible military combat situation during his many conquests. Every time he stepped into the gladiator arena, however, he encountered situations that were completely new and unfamiliar to him. Strange opponents, exotic animals, and a crowd baying for blood, all combined to create a Volatile, Uncertain, Complex, and Ambiguous environment.

As he fought for his life, did Maximus primarily rely on his gut to find the answers, or did he lean on his mates to find the best path to victory? Were his fighters intimidated by his larger-than-life persona, or were they comfortable jumping in and taking the lead when they knew something unique to the situation?

I think that Maximus could not have survived the odds by purely operating from the gut and screaming orders from the top. To achieve consistent success, he would have built a *tight-knit unit of equals* who *deeply trusted each other*, and *selflessly adopted the best of their pooled knowledge* to navigate each encounter.

I saw some of these behaviors in action on that summer day of team building. They are the same behaviors we must foster within our workplace to survive the next disruption.

3.1 THE IMPORTANCE OF FRICTION

In the physical world, friction is defined as the resistance an object encounters when it moves against another one. Most people think of friction as something deleterious, a force that slows us down and makes us work harder to achieve the same objective. But it is also essential for enabling things like transportation (wheels are useless if they cannot get traction on the road) and walking (try to walk on a floor covered with oil).

In the human context, friction is equated with conflict. It is the pushback you experience when your opinion encounters a contrary one from another person.

When you encounter friction, you have two options. You can try to understand your opponent's point of view and work with them to remove the friction. Or you can use brute force to overrule the other person and keep moving forward.

Is friction in human interactions a good thing? Just like in the physical world, it depends. If friction results in better outcomes, then it is undoubtedly a good thing. If the person slowing you down has something useful to offer, then it can be mutually beneficial to both parties.

That said, promoting good friction between people is not easy. All it takes is a few bad interactions to turn them off for good. For example, if a person is regularly over-ruled, or worse, penalized for sharing their frank opinions, they will settle into a path of least resistance and just go with what the other person wants.

When people stop pushing back, they come to every discussion saying exactly what the other person wants to hear. This is especially true when there is a power imbalance. People who fear their boss tend to quickly retract statements when there is the slightest indication of pushback. Even when the boss says something controversial or crazy, everyone just nods and agrees. For the boss, it can feel so smooth, so *frictionless*! There is a better word to describe the situation – *apathy*.

When no one pushes back, it is a sure sign that people have stopped caring and are just going through the motions. Is that the kind of environment you want to operate in?

Conversely, what does it look like when leaders nurture friction and actively go out seeking it? They end up with a culture where people speak up and actively contribute to discussions.

In a high feedback environment, people do not wait to be asked for information but instead seek out their leaders to surface issues and problems. They come to work every day with clarity of purpose and see it as their personal mission to help their enterprise succeed. In my previous company, we called these types of people *shiny-eyed*.

In the previous chapters, we discussed the importance of setting a clear north star, aligning incentives, and operating bottoms-up. If you do this well, you will have at your disposal a focused and nimble army that operates with speed and works in a highly autonomous manner. That said, as you navigate your next crisis or disruption, you are certain to encounter unanticipated and unfamiliar roadblocks that challenge your knowledge and assumptions. What kind of environment would you prefer to operate in when that happens? A low-friction one where you are all alone in making critical decisions, or a high-friction one where diverse opinions challenge and augment your assumptions?

Rep. John Lewis[9] had a famous quote: "Never, ever be afraid to make some noise and get in good trouble." Inpowering Leaders actively look for "good trouble." They embrace the many voices in their organization and encourage them to speak up. They give people not only the opportunity to be in the room but also play in the game.

Leaders who operate this way create a culture of honest decision-making backed by the best possible data. They are the ones best equipped to survive change and disruption.

3.2 CREATING A HIGH FEEDBACK ENVIRONMENT

All through my career, I was always a continuous improvement enthusiast, with a habit of noting down opportunities when I saw them. Every so often, I would pause to examine my collection of ideas, prioritize them

---

[9] John Robert Lewis was an American politician and civil-rights leader

for impact, and take the top ones forward for implementation. I was quite successful in using this approach to launch and execute numerous self-improvement projects. When I tried to scale it beyond myself, however, I went through a painful process that taught me some valuable lessons.

My company had a corporate-level operating system that everyone was expected to use in their daily lives. A foundational tool within this system was the Quality Control Process Clinic (QCPC). We made a list of all the things our organization did, chose a few that had the highest impact on our customers, and then set up a system to collect turnbacks[10] that we regularly analyzed to make improvements.

QCPC has its roots in a Japanese quality system that was brought over to our company by an expert name Yuzuru Ito[11]. It works quite well in the factory environment where operators keep a log of what went wrong at each production machine, sort the information into buckets (like "shutdown," "bad dimension," "jammed tool"), and then perform in-depth analysis to find systematic improvement opportunities. The critical enabler of success is data – if you have lots of data, you can develop richer insights and identify higher impact improvements.

---

[10] A turnback is anything that stops you or slows you down in delivering to your customer.
[11] Mr. Yuzuru Ito was the Quality Vice President at Matsushita Electric and later a consultant in the US.

Since production machines handle many parts and assemblies every day, there is always a treasure trove of data available at the end of the week. Unfortunately, when I tried to implement the same methods in a white-collar office environment, my organization generated very little data. It was baffling because I knew that we regularly encountered issues in our daily work. So why were people not logging turnbacks?

I started investigating and learned three reasons for our situation.

1. The process of entering turnbacks was cumbersome. You had to log into the tool, find your project, and then enter not only the turnback but also a bunch of additional "nice-to-have" information to make it easier for the person who managed the database. It was enough to turn off even the most enthusiastic submitter. Our learning from this was: *if you do not make it easy for people to provide feedback, they will likely pass on the opportunity*.

2. Some people were not comfortable with the *idea* of entering turnbacks. One person I spoke with told me that logging a turnback was rude. It was like confronting the person who owned the process and telling them that what they were doing was wrong. I was surprised by this comment. All along, I had assumed that people would see the value of logging turnbacks because that would help everyone improve. However, if turnbacks were considered a personal affront,

then it was highly unlikely that people would participate. This taught us another key lesson: *to drive more feedback, we needed to destigmatize the process of giving it.* We had to build a culture where people saw feedback as data that targeted a <u>process</u> and not a <u>person</u>.

3. People could not connect their efforts to outcomes. Many of them told us that they had diligently submitted turnbacks, but then heard nothing. It seemed like their inputs were just going into a black hole, leaving little motivation to submit even more turnbacks. This taught us our third lesson: *to stay motivated, people had to see the fruits of their labor.*

The above three lessons critically informed our approach for improving QCPC. We ran numerous information sessions where we emphasized the importance of data for continuous improvement. We made several changes to the turnback submission process to make it convenient and easy. We closed the loop by communicating the improvements that were implemented based on the submitted turnbacks. These three actions increased participation, leading to more turnback data, hence enabling the cycle of continuous improvement to continue.

I was fascinated by how much the above lessons overlapped with everything I had learned as a manager. In every assignment, my success had been correlated with my effectiveness in collecting accurate data to inform my decisions. It made me realize the importance of creating a culture that encouraged people to disagree with me and augment my knowledge. You had to destigmatize and encourage feedback, you had to make it easy for people to provide it, and you had to show positive outcomes so that they would keep doing it.

3.3 DESTIGMATIZING FEEDBACK

Do you watch reality TV? There was a time when I used to watch "American Idol." The show featured a group of talented singers who belted out crowd favorites and tried to garner the most votes from listeners.

A panel of three judges judged each performance. One of them, whose name was Simon Cowell, was a bit of a curmudgeon. The other two judges always tried to be nice, even after a bad performance. Simon, on the other hand, said it exactly as he saw it. If he thought the performance was bad, he told the contestant exactly what he thought of their effort and what they must do to improve.

Who do you think was helping the contestants improve as singers? And who did the crowd boo?

We are trained and conditioned from birth to be nice to others. It is an endearing trait that goes a long way in making our social interactions positive and uplifting. As Gautama Buddha said: "It is sometimes better to be kind than to be right."

In many situations, the difference in outcome is too small, and we choose to take the path of kindness and let things go. That said, if caring for others' feelings prevents us from communicating critical information that could be the difference between life and death, then some behavioral adjustments might be in order.

In today's fast-paced business environment, time is of the essence. There is simply no bandwidth for missteps and diversions. To move forward with speed <u>and</u> accuracy, you must surround yourself with people who are willing to offer the truth, no matter how painful or inconvenient. It is better to acknowledge reality and prepare for the worst, than to bury your head in the sand and hope those things will go away.

When a person pushes back and provides an alternate point of view, it should not be seen as an affront. Instead, it should be viewed as an act of caring.

A person who pushes back puts themselves in a vulnerable spot. If they are willing to do it, they likely have reasonable justification, and it is incumbent on others to listen and probe further. It is vital that such conversations be polite and civil. I have seen too many instances where people with valuable information destroy their credibility by making snide remarks. Such situations must be managed immediately, visibly, and firmly.

Leaders must *actively* foster a culture of respect where *everyone* invited into a discussion has an equal voice and gets to express their thoughts without judgment. People who disagree should not have to couch their feedback in diplomatic language. They should be able to speak directly, and rest assured that their input will be taken at face value without assumptions of malice.

Getting to the above state is not always easy, especially in organizations with tenured staff who may carry baggage from past experiences. As a leader, you will need to show the way. You will need to consistently display a mindset that focuses on the message and not the messenger.

Every time someone pushes back on you, you will need to hold judgment, try not to defend, and instead probe further. You will need to offer the floor and adopt an exploratory style. By acting this way often enough, you will build an environment where people drop their defenses and treat contrary inputs as data, not criticism. Once they become comfortable pushing back on their leader, they will also become comfortable pushing back on their peers. As this culture of free speech takes hold, it will unleash your team's inner potential and bring out their best ideas.

A great way to encourage feedback is through recognition. By visibly praising instances when someone adjusts your worldview, you will break down the barrier between managers and subordinates. You will get one step closer to a relationship where people in your team think they work *with you* rather than *for you*.

Another way to encourage feedback is to eliminate this word from your vocabulary. The word *feedback* has negative connotations for too many people. It is better to talk in terms of *data*, treat all inputs as *suggestions*, explore a range of *opportunities*, and emphasize how all this extra *information* empowers you to become better and stronger.

Please stop here and reflect on the culture of feedback in your organization. As you answer the following questions, think about what you can do to make every interaction a meaningful learning experience.

1. Think back to some of your recent meetings. How vibrant were the discussions? Did the proceedings feel scripted, or did people actively engage and politely challenge each other?

2. Can you recall a meeting where you came out thinking quite differently from how you felt when you went in? What enabled that to happen?

3. What can you do to make people more comfortable with pushing back on you as well as each other?

4. Do you have highly knowledgeable and opinionated "Simons" in your organization? How have you harnessed and channeled them to your advantage?

Timeout

Welcome back. I hope this timeout helped you think about ways to create a data-rich environment at your workplace. This will be critical for generating high quality inputs when you make decisions.

Once you have built a culture of speaking up, the next important step is to encourage your people to *proactively* find you when they get into trouble. This approach will allow you to render help and execute pivots quickly.

3.4 ENCOURAGING BAD NEWS

When things go wrong, the best thing people can do is ask for help. Many people do not proactively seek help, however, because their leaders have a management style that discourages bad news. Instead, they stay quiet and spin their wheels, looking for ways to fix the situation on their own. *This kind of behavior is pure waste.* It can be the worst enemy when an organization is trying to move with speed.

I used to regularly remind my team that *bad news is good news* when promptly communicated because it allows others to come in and help fix the situation. Bad news becomes terrible news, however, when it is not shared. In such cases, the team can spend too much time spinning their wheels and end up in situations from which they cannot recover.

Most people agree, in principle, that they should speak the truth. The trick lies in making them do it.

When people are uncomfortable with conveying the truth, they use their next best option – silence. Have you ever been in a bad situation where the leader lamented that no one had said anything in past meetings?

Some projects and initiatives implode not because the people working on them are unaware of the issues, but because they choose to not let their bosses know. As a leader, you must avoid such situations at all costs. You must establish a culture where your people speak up and let you know the truth. You must show again and again, through actions, not words, that bad news is not only tolerated but indeed encouraged. This requires mental preparation and deliberate action. It also requires humility.

To build a culture that encourages bad news, you will need to walk into difficult and contentious conversations ready to listen, willing to empathize, and being laser-focused on solving the problem. By operating this way, you will build trust and create buy-in. Even when you make an unpopular decision, your team will appreciate that their input was acknowledged and considered.

Keep in mind that you will not get this right every time. What will go a long way, however, is your attitude and your willingness to learn.

On numerous occasions during my career, I reconsidered decisions after the fact. After a particularly contentious meeting, I would seek out the people who had challenged my thinking and re-engaged them to take another look. Sometimes I changed my mind, and sometimes I did not. However, I think my willingness to reconsider encouraged people to come back next time and speak the truth.

Here is the bottom line: even in the best of times, the speed with which you escalate bad news and fix situations can be the difference between success and failure. In the worst of times, it can be the difference between survival and extinction.

Inpowering Leaders work hard to set up a strong culture of truth and honesty even during times of "peace." Having this foundation in place enables them to be truly ready when they engage in their next serious "war."

Please stop here and take another timeout. As you answer the following questions, think about what you can do to encourage the people in your organization to tell you the truth, no matter how untimely or inconvenient.

1. How do you usually react to bad news? Do you feel that your people advise you quickly and honestly when things are not going well?

2. How do your project and organizational scorecards look? Are they full of "greens" or are there also some "reds" in the mix? Do you regularly find a mismatch between your data and what the people on the ground are saying?

3. Think about a recent incident when your team communicated information that did not gel with

what you were expecting to hear. Did you acknowledge the situation and work with your team to resolve it, or did you send them back to rework the information and come back with something better aligned with your expectations? How did it all play out in the end?

4. Do you think your people fear you as a leader? If yes, how can you reset the tone and messaging in your interactions to make people more comfortable with proactively approaching you and speaking the truth?

Timeout

Welcome back. I hope you reflected on your operating style and thought of ways to make your people comfortable speaking the truth. The existence of your enterprise may depend on it someday.

Now that we have set the foundation for open and honest communications, it is time to discuss the reinforcement loop of communicating outcomes, an area of opportunity in most organizations.

3.5 CLOSING THE LOOP ON OUTCOMES

I was on my semi-annual circuit through Europe to visit various engineering facilities in my organization. It was a warm summer day, and I was speaking to a group of engineers seated inside a large conference hall. I had requested this all-hands meeting to share the latest business developments and their relevance to the local team's work.

I gave a brief overview of the business and then spent the rest of my time describing specific projects on which the local engineers were working. Before ending, I talked about an initiative that they had supported a couple of years ago. I explained how their work had benefited the company and driven significant business outcomes. I concluded by reminding everyone of the importance of their work and how critical their contributions were to the company's long-term success.

After the meeting was over, one of the attendees approached me and said how happy he was to hear that the project he had worked on two years before had made a positive impact on the business. He was the project leader and had not heard anything since the project was completed. He got great satisfaction and inspiration from hearing that he and his team had made such a difference to the company.

This incident made me think. The person I had just spoken with was quite senior and well-connected within the company. Even so, he did not know the impact his project had made to the business. His team had put in a lot of hard work but had not enjoyed the satisfaction that came from seeing success at the end. What a lost opportunity for reinforcement! If people could connect their work with its business impact, imagine how much more inspired they would be and how much harder they would push to achieve success.

Have you experienced anything like this at your workplace? Do people sincerely toil away on things that their leaders ask them to work on but never get to hear about the outcomes?

As you attempt to build a culture of open communication *during* projects and initiatives, you must drive a similar culture *after the fact*. Irrespective of whether things succeed or not, you must close the loop with stakeholders so that they can savor the wins and learn from the losses.

When people see the connection between their work and its outcomes, they become enthusiastic and ready to jump into their next activity. Feeding this curiosity is an essential element of Inpowering Leadership.

I would like you to take a short timeout here and think about your organization's culture of looking back. As you answer the following questions, think about how you can use retrospectives as a tool for reinforcement and learning.

1. How would you rate your organization's effectiveness in closing the loop on projects and initiatives? Does your team have a good idea of how their actions are creating business impact?

2. Do you have a formal process for performing retrospectives? If yes, what range of activities do you perform retrospectives on, and do they cover all aspects of work performed by your organization? If not, how can you get going on this?

Timeout

Welcome back. I hope you were able to think of ways to foster a culture of learning from past experiences. Organizations that perform high-quality retrospectives become stronger and more resilient over time. They use the learnings to make systemic improvements and reinforce institutional memory, which can be critical enablers during a disruption.

So far, in this chapter, we have discussed how you can build a culture of open communication where people push back and tell you the truth. In the next sections, we will discuss techniques by which you can reach deeper into your organization and seek out even more data to inform your decisions. These techniques are essential for calibrating your assumptions, especially as you gain seniority and move further away from people who perform the actual work on the ground.

3.6 SEEKING (GOOD) TROUBLE

I advise a startup company that develops innovative technologies to remove harmful chemicals from water. When I started, I was new to the water industry and explored numerous avenues to learn about this space.

One of my ex-colleagues introduced me to Vince Caprio, a public policy expert who drives initiatives to upgrade the aging water supply infrastructure in the US. My first conversation with him was quite memorable. Vince jumped right in and inundated me with all sorts of information on the water industry: how it works, who the key players are, and what it takes to bring new technologies into this highly regulated and conservative market.

For the first 15 minutes, I felt like I was drinking from a firehose. At some point, Vince figured this out and apologized for drowning me in all the information. He was aware that our startup was run by a young chemical engineer who did not have a lot of industry experience. He was merely trying to help me understand the context we were operating in so that we could develop robust plans that did not suffer from blind spots.

Vince then proceeded to tell me a story from his other passion – nanotechnology – that vividly illustrated what can happen when people operate inside an information bubble. The nanotechnology business went through a boom in the early 2000s, with many startup companies sprouting up all over the place. These companies were run by technically gifted researchers who had developed proprietary chemicals with the potential to transform a wide range of industries from biopharma to semiconductors.

In 2005, nanotech was considered the next great technology wave. But the hype fizzled away over the next few years, and the companies either closed shop pivoted into something else

One of the reasons for the nanotech debacle was that many of the founders had not figured out an economical way to manufacture their wonder chemicals at scale. Although their ideas were brilliant, the products could not be brought to market viably.

Why did so many companies suffer a similar fate? One reason was that these companies did not have experienced management teams who could accurately flag the risks posed by this product viability gap. As a result, 1.5 billion dollars of venture money went down the tubes.

I wish the above story were an anomaly. Unfortunately, it is not the case. More than half of all startups in the US shutter within the first four years of incorporation. In a survey by Fast Company, the top reason cited by entrepreneurs for their startup's failure was that they did not have the right team with the diversity of knowledge required for success.

Just think about this. Startups, by definition, attempt something difficult that no one else is doing. Their success depends on making high-quality decisions in an inherently uncertain environment. Their teams are small and bottoms-up in their thinking. Their frugal resources drive a culture of accountability. With all these operating strengths, the only thing they lack is *data*.

Vince figured out that I was the designated gray beard in our water purification startup and was on a deliberate mission to collect more data. And boy, did he deliver! He gave me lots of new information, filling in critical knowledge gaps that could be the difference between success and failure.

When you lead your organization in a rapidly changing environment, you can feel a lot like a founder in a startup. You regularly face new and unfamiliar situations that are outside your past experiences. The only way to survive is to collect more data. You must not only encourage the people within your team to speak up but also step out of your bubble and seek other sources of information. *You must go looking for trouble.*

3.7 OUTBOUND ENGAGEMENT

Over the years, I have used a variety of engagement models to accumulate data. They broadly fall into two categories – outbound engagement and inbound engagement.

In the outbound approach, I proactively engage people who can offer new perspectives and challenge my assumptions. This approach relies entirely on my initiative. I go about it in two ways – specific and exploratory.

The *specific* approach is opportunistic. I use it when working on new and challenging problems where I want a different set of eyes. I set up small slots of time with various people and get their feedback on my thinking. The mix of people depends heavily on the topic at hand. It could include team members, stakeholders, customers, and sometimes even close friends and family. An essential requirement is that the people I speak with must have some skin in the game. They must care about the outcomes enough to provide honest feedback.

I have deployed the *specific* engagement approach on numerous technical and business problems. One incident from early in my career showed me how effective this approach could be in non-technical situations as well. Four years into my tenure at our company's corporate research center, I got the opportunity to move to one of the business units. The assignment came with a promotion and set high expectations. I was both excited and intimidated. I decided to get some other perspectives before I made my decision.

I spoke with many of my peers, superiors, and mentors. Although everyone gave me pros and cons, they were mostly bullish about the opportunity and encouraged me to go for it. All these people had worked closely with me and were confident that I would find a way to meet the new role's high expectations.

One conversation went in the opposite direction, however. A senior leader told me that this would be a terrible move that would set me up for certain failure. He painted a scary picture where I would be mauled by senior management because of my lack of experience and political acumen. He advised me that I should stay put in my current job, where I was surrounded by well-wishers who would support me when things went wrong and give me time to grow at my own pace.

I was at first taken aback and upset. After some reflection, however, I felt quite glad to have had this conversation. This leader had provided me with an unvarnished view of all the things that could go wrong. It helped me more accurately calibrate if I was ready for my new assignment. It also injected a little extra energy into me – I now had a point to prove and worked just that bit harder to be successful.

Another outbound approach I use for engaging people is *exploratory*. It is usually in the form of open-ended conversations. The whole point is to increase access to new people and leverage it as a learning tool.

One method I have used quite successfully is the monthly "straight talk" meeting. A randomly selected group of ten to fifteen people from my organization sit around a table (sometimes with coffee and snacks) and talk about how things are going. To ensure that people speak their mind, I check beforehand that no two people in the room are in a reporting relationship.

I usually break the ice by saying that I am mainly

there to listen and learn, and whatever we discuss will stay in the room. Things usually start out slow, but we always end up in a free-flowing conversation by the end. I am constantly surprised by the unexpected quarters from where I learn the most impactful things. The quietest people in the room ask some of the most challenging questions and offer some of the pithiest observations.

Another exploratory method I have used effectively is to walk around the facility and talk with people at their work locations[12]. Meeting people at their "home base" makes them relax. It also allows other innocent bystanders to walk up and join the conversation.

Another great technique that I never mastered but have seen other leaders do well is the lunch table conversation. This approach creates an opportunity for people to engage in informal settings and talk more freely. Whenever I have used it, I have been able to get a better pulse of how the organization is doing.

I cannot recommend the exploratory method enough. It gives the rank and file an opportunity to interact with their leader and speak their mind. It also helps the leader with discovering hidden gems in their organization. I have used this technique with success not only in the US but also in India,[13] where people are usually less willing to discuss issues in an open forum.

---

[12] This technique is also referred to as Management By Walking Around.

[13] In India, we called this forum "Chat with Leader".

3.8 INBOUND ENGAGEMENT

While outbound engagement is a way to go out and seek data, inbound engagement is a way to make the data find you. In this approach, people in the organization take the initiative to engage their leader and provide (sometimes unsolicited) advice.

I must say that whenever this happened to me, it was pure joy. I was surprised repeatedly by who walked into my office and what they told me. You would think that the inbound approach would predominantly attract complainers and whiners. But a healthy portion of the walk-ins and pop-ins were people who had digested the organization's mission and were interested in actively contributing to its success.

Some of my most memorable conversations happened in the aftermath of "all-hands" meetings. People would walk in upset and concerned about something that one of the presenters had said. After I investigated a little, I would usually discover that some of the comments had been unclear and hence misinterpreted. I sometimes also found that the presentation contained imprecise and confusing language. This was my chance to clarify, and once I had done so, my colleagues would start to immediately feel better. As they left my office, I asked that they communicate my clarifications to all their friends as well.

There were occasions when people showed up without warning and asked if we could talk. Some of these people came in with well thought out agendas, complete with problem statements and suggestions. Others just showed up with a jumble of ideas in their heads that I had to extract through conversation. I got advice on topics that ranged from solving short term issues to setting long-term strategy. I even once had a person tell me that I was not the right person for my job!

These incidents grew my knowledge and helped me improve the quality of my decisions. They also provided validation that I had created an environment where (at least some) people felt comfortable enough to challenge me proactively.

This type of inbound engagement is not easy to create. To foster it, you must do two things. The first is knowledge dissemination. You must ensure that everyone is aware of the challenges the company is trying to solve so they can organically generate and contribute their ideas. This was already covered in the last chapter[14], so I will not repeat it here. The second thing you must do is be approachable and display openness to new information. It is intimidating for employees to approach their superiors, especially those that are multiple levels above them. As a leader, it is incumbent on you to create a welcoming, non-threatening, and intellectually curious environment that encourages people to find you and provide unsolicited advice.

You can start by reminding people that your door is

---

[14] Please see the section on Operating Bottoms-up.

always open, and you are always looking for new ideas. I did this at the end of every interaction and staff meeting.

The next thing you can do is to make sure that people can physically get to you without attracting too much attention. Unfortunately, this is something that I did not pay enough attention to when I first became a VP. I sat in a corner office in a zoned off area where the only way for someone to get to me was by walking past a set of glass-walled offices and then through my administrative assistant, who would, at the minimum, ask them why they wanted to meet me. In hindsight, the whole setup was somewhat intimidating, even if unintentional.

One day I was having a farewell conversation with an engineer who was about to retire. I asked him what I could do better, and he said, "Please change the design of your office." My first reaction was that of surprise. As he elaborated, however, I understood what he was saying. I thanked him for shining a light on an apparent blind spot and proceeded to implement changes that made the overall space more open and welcoming. I changed the layout of my office and sat directly in front of the door to make immediate eye contact with visitors. I also moved my administrative assistant to a corner and ensured that she no longer acted as a gatekeeper.

The last and perhaps most important thing you must do is create an environment of respect and empathy. When someone takes the initiative to come and talk with you, it is usually motivated by pain, or caring, or a combination of the two. It is best to adopt an exploratory style during your conversation and give the other person the time and space they need to get their points across. If you cannot afford this, it is better to reschedule than just go through the motions.

Remember that word gets around. Reputations, like trees, take a long time to nurture and only a few minutes to destroy. You need only one or two incidents where people feel like they did not get your attention or respect, and the well of information will completely dry up.

I would like you to stop here and take a timeout. As you answer the following questions, think about how you can actively seek (good) trouble and use all the resources at your disposal to collect more information.

1. What approach do you use to collect more information, especially when working on things that are outside your expertise? How far and wide do you cast your net? Do you always go to the same people, or does the mix change depending on the problem? How can you become more effective at this?

2. What channels have you created for people to access you informally? Do you feel that people are comfortable with approaching you and can easily find you?

3. Have you had any illuminating conversations in the recent past that occurred because someone

from your team approached you? What did you do to create a welcoming environment? How did you ensure that the conversations were honest?

4. What additional steps could you take to increase the quantity and quality of inbound engagement you see? Is this something you value and look forward to? Why, or why not?

Timeout

Welcome back. I hope you thought of ways to increase your engagement with the people in your organization. It will not only give you new insights but also help you with building stronger relationships.

We are now ready to discuss another tool that can help you increase the accuracy of your decisions – diversity.

3.9 THE POWER OF DIVERSE THINKING

A few years ago, I was at an uncertain point in my career. Our company had gone through some changes at the top. Some of my mentors had left, and I was dealing with a new set of leaders who did not know anything about me.

When I met my new manager, I described who I was, where I was going, and what I hoped would happen in the coming months and years. He was sympathetic to my situation and asked me to stay tuned as he explored options for my next assignment. I felt relieved and went back to work, full of energy and enthusiasm.

I heard nothing. Days became weeks, and weeks started to become months. I assumed that my new boss was working behind the scenes and would soon contact me.

Then one day, I spoke with a trusted colleague who saw the world through a different lens. He heard my story and immediately said, "If you have heard nothing, then you need to assume that no one has done anything." His take on the issue was jarring. It took some time for me to process what he was saying. Soon, however, I realized that he was right. My manager was extremely busy, and it was unlikely that he saw my situation with the same level of urgency as I did. If I wanted to move things along, I would have to take direct control.

I started making phone calls and worked with my some of my contacts to conceive and finalize my next assignment. It was not what I had originally targeted, but it was a reasonable compromise, given the circumstances. Most importantly, it allowed me to move on with my life.

In the chapter on self-awareness, I talked about how our belief systems can create blind spots. The above story was a vivid illustration of one of my blind spots. Somehow, due to my optimistic nature, I could not see something that was in plain sight for my colleague.

This incident was an aha (!) moment for me. It showed me in a very personal way that the same information can evoke very different insights when exposed to people who have had different life experiences. In short, it showed me the power of *diverse thinking*.

So far, in this chapter, we have discussed techniques by which you can create an inclusive culture where people speak up and challenge your assumptions. We have also discussed the use of outbound and inbound engagement to increase the amount of data that informs your decisions. Our next topic of discussion is diversity – a technique that can help you further enrich the quality of your data.

Diversity is based on the premise that when you search for new insights, there is no point talking with people who think just like you. To truly pressure test your assumptions, you must bounce your ideas with people who view the world differently. Decisions that pass such pressure tests are likely to be more accurate.

3.10 FOSTERING DIVERSITY

Diversity is a hot topic today. Every company worth its salt has put out statements that emphasize its commitment to a diverse and inclusive workforce.

A 2013 Harvard Business Review article revealed that 85% of companies with annual income above $500 million recognize diversity as a key driver of innovation. That said, organizations have struggled to deliver on this promise. Although some have managed to hire diverse talent, I have seen few success stories where this structural advantage has been converted into meaningful outcomes.

Let us take a step back and think about this afresh. What is diversity? My definition is: *not like me (or us)*.

Diversity is not just about race, color, and gender. Diversity can be achieved through many other vectors such as culture, religion, nationality, sexual orientation, political views, and socioeconomic backgrounds, to name a few. When melded together, these can create a unique tapestry of knowledge, beliefs, and values.

Every organization contains a particular mix of experiences. As the world changes, leaders must continuously analyze their population and determine what new perspectives can be added to make *tangible impacts* on business outcomes. This should be a deliberate exercise with participation from the broader organization in discussions and setting targets.

All too often, however, companies default to a top-down approach where diversity targets are set at the corporate level and then cascaded down, without any consideration of individual needs or circumstances at the lower levels of the organization. No matter how well-meaning the initiative is, if not implemented properly, it can result in little buy-in and adoption on the ground.

It does not end there. Even if the organization succeeds in hiring diverse talent, they might find that the people they worked so hard to hire are struggling to assimilate and integrate. If the hiring team never saw these people's value in the first place, they will likely not be open to the ideas and opinions they bring. Over time, the new hires will become disillusioned, their morale will suffer, and some of them will eventually leave. This is a theme that is playing out across many industries.

Building a diverse workforce is *not easy*. The whole point of diversity is to bring in new points of view that challenge our assumptions. This cannot be implemented in a vacuum. It must sit within a continuum of deliberate actions.

Before you start hiring diverse talent, you must build an inclusive culture where the people on your team feel like they have a voice. You should include them in the process of developing your diversity targets. This will force everyone to get aligned on the rationale behind diversity and create buy-in for targets that are set. This buy-in will, in turn, motivate the assimilation process because your team will be eager to benefit from the knowledge of the newcomers. Once the new people are in, your culture of openness will allow their ideas and opinions to be accepted and even welcomed. The flywheel of diversity will gain momentum with every hiring and assimilation cycle and eventually become a part of your DNA.

You may have noticed that inclusion is a prerequisite for the above process. *Only after you have built an inclusive culture can you truly take on the challenge of increasing your organization's diversity.* This is the opposite of what we commonly hear in the industry, where it is described as "Diversity & Inclusion." I think we must move instead to a paradigm of "Inclusion, then Diversity."

The best diversity targets are the ones that everyone can understand and get behind. People are not as selfish and protective of their turf as you might think. Everyone wants to be part of a winning team. If you include them in the process, you will likely end up with sensible targets that everyone supports and feels accountable to.

Please stop here to introspect and reflect. As you answer the following questions, think about the current state of diversity in your organization and what you can do to enhance it.

1. Do you feel that your team has the right variety of experiences (both professional and personal) that you need to be successful in today's business environment? What vectors of diversity could you add to help you become more effective as a leader? As you think about this, I recommend comparing your formative experiences and belief

systems with those of the people on your team.

2. What personal attributes do you look for when you interview people? When was the last time you hired someone whose thinking style and life experiences were very different from yours?

3. Do you have diversity targets today? Do you agree with them? How aligned are your team members with these expectations?

4. What can you do to speed up the diversity flywheel in your organization?

⧗ Timeout

Welcome back. I hope you developed some actions to add diversity to your organization and create tangible business outcomes. I highly recommend that you partner with your team as you take these actions forward.

We are now in the home stretch. The techniques we have discussed so far in this chapter will help you create a data-rich environment where people actively engage you and feed you knowledge and insights. After you have done all this hard work with your team, the last steps in the journey are entirely yours.

3.11 OPENING UP TO NEW POINTS OF VIEW

Let us revisit the nanotechnology story from earlier in this chapter. When I first heard it, I was convinced that fundamental blind spots had scuppered this highly promising industry. However, on further reflection, I could not help feeling that there was more to this story.

At the peak of the nanotechnology boom, there were around 1,200 startups worldwide, with over a billion dollars of venture money invested. How was it possible that *so many founders* and *so many venture capitalists* had overlooked the manufacturing challenges with these chemicals?

I thought back to some of the complex projects that I had worked on during my career. Had there been any instances where we were fully aware of insurmountable issues but kept going because we thought that with just a little more creativity and hard work, we would be able to get across the finish line? The answer, unfortunately, is yes. I sense that something similar likely also happened in the nano industry.

Leaders who accumulate many successes and persevere through many challenges develop an inordinately strong belief that they can get through any situation, no matter the circumstances. This type of thinking is especially prevalent in venture capitalists, many of whom have successfully founded and scaled enterprises. This *illusion of control* can make them keep going in the face of conflicting information and make them waste a lot of time and resources before they finally decide to stop and honestly acknowledge the situation.

When I was an engineering leader, I was asked on numerous occasions to build innovative products with technology that was not ready. After a few failures, I developed a guiding rule for these conversations: "If it is just a matter of working hard, we can probably find a way to get there. If it is a matter of overcoming unsolved physics, all bets are off." I cannot claim to have won every battle. I have a few impressive scars from the ones I lost.

Risk-taking is in the blood of leaders. It is something we are naturally wired for and incentivized to do. I, too, have been guilty on many occasions of disregarding all sorts of warning signs. But I have learned from those experiences.

I have learned that when my team passionately pushes back on me and has the data to justify it, it is incumbent on me to take a step back and make an effort to listen. At that point, my job as the leader becomes one of opening my mind to alternate worldviews and ingesting as much information as possible.

Like me, you too are programmed to lean on pre-existing intuitions and beliefs. To lead successfully in times of change, you will need to actively suppress these tendencies. You will need to create an internal calm, and truly listen to what is being said by others. You will need to enter conversations with your brain resembling *Tabula Rasa*, absent of preconceived ideas or predetermined goals, and ready to accept new knowledge. If you become effective at this, it will be your most remarkable talent.

A complementary tool that will help you is reflection. I made poor decisions on numerous occasions when I was unable to hold back my preconceived notions. After leaving meetings that had been particularly rocky, I tried to replay the high friction moments and re-evaluate my decisions. If my calmer mind told me something was amiss, I went back, re-convened the group, re-discussed the information, and changed my decision when appropriate.

All of us possess the ability to keep our "antennas up" and pick up on friction when it occurs. The best response is to recognize it immediately and listen more carefully. However, we are all human and can sometimes find it challenging to suppress our biases in the heat of the moment. When that happens, the next best path is to reflect afterward and correct the outcome. Every time you do this, two things will happen. First, you will get onto a more reliable path for success. Second, your organization will become a little more emboldened to speak up because it made a difference the last time they tried.

It is time for another timeout. As you answer the following questions, think about how you can overcome your biases and truly open your mind to new learnings.

1. How do you think the people in your team would

describe your approach to interactive discourse? Where would they put you on the spectrum from "my way or the highway" to "help me find the right way"? Do you think you are well-calibrated on this?

2. Would you consider yourself as someone who actively seeks to challenge your worldview? How well do you react to critical input from people who are below you in the reporting chain?

3. If you could work on improving one thing in your listening style, what would that be, and how would you go about it?

⧗ Timeout

Welcome back. I hope you took some time to reflect on your listening style, specifically how you can slow down your judgment, *objectively listen* to the people around you, and use their inputs to make *honest decisions*.

One last technique I would like to discuss before closing this chapter is the "strategic timeout." It has been an essential part of my toolkit and might benefit you as well.

3.12 STRATEGIC TIMEOUTS

It was late on a Wednesday evening. I was mentally exhausted, but also happy with what I had achieved. I would never have got this much done if I had gone in to work.

It was one of my "off" days when I had blocked my calendar and spent the day working from home. This was a practice that I had experimented with and formalized during my early years as a manager. It allowed me to reflect and focus deeply without interruptions.

Like other off days, this one had started out slow. It took me about three hours in the morning to answer my emails and pull my mind out of the daily firefights. Then I jumped into the project of the day – drafting a multi-year strategic plan.

It took me a couple of hours to sort and analyze the information I had collected over the past months. Once I had done the setup work, the ideas started to flow.

By late in the day, I was inside a cone of silence, with only my thoughts and cups of tea for company. When I finally got up in the evening, I had a draft I could take to my team for further discussion.

These types of deliberately scheduled "strategic timeout" sessions are my growth engine. They enable me to slow down, step back, and see the forest for the trees. They create bandwidth to process recent events, synthesize learnings, and use them to drive strategic planning activities.

Whenever I have such sessions, they result in growth for both my organization and me. When I am not able to make time for them, I go through phases of stagnation.

I have seen some variants of this approach. Some leaders block out chunks of time on their calendar for unplanned discussions. Others prefer to host offsites with formal agendas. In the end, the idea is always the same – get away from the daily firefights, spend some time reflecting, synthesize new insights, and develop high-quality long-term plans.

Please pause here and take a timeout. As you answer the following questions, think about how you can create bandwidth for thinking and reflection.

1. How deliberate are you with including strategic timeouts in your schedule? Do you consider this practice helpful? If yes, why? If not, why not?

2. Can you readily estimate what percentage of time you spend on strategic planning and continuous improvement activities? Do you think this is adequate? What can you do to bring a better balance between tactical and strategic activities?

Timeout

Welcome back. That was the last timeout of the chapter. It was also a fitting culmination to our discussion around learning and reflection.

As a leader, you must think not only about today but also about tomorrow, and the day after. As your organization starts moving with intent towards its North Star, it is incumbent on you to figure out what lies beyond it. Strategic timeouts will help you in this quest.

CHAPTER SUMMARY

In this chapter, we discussed how you can increase the accuracy of your decisions. In today's fast-changing world, there will be many situations when you will not have the answers. To make accurate decisions, you will need to rapidly collect new information from diverse sources and build a more comprehensive dataset.

We started the chapter with a discussion on friction and pushback. We explored ways by which you can build a culture where people speak up and challenge each other's opinions. We also discussed how you can destigmatize the idea of giving feedback and encourage everyone to proactively ask for help.

Next, we introduced the concept of seeking "good trouble" by stepping out and soliciting information. We discussed two methods – outbound engagement, where you directly engage people to learn from them, and inbound engagement, where people come and find you to offer their inputs.

With these foundations in place, we explored another essential tool to enrich your data – diversity. We discussed how you can build diverse organizations that make meaningful impacts on business outcomes. We also discussed the importance of opening your mind to effectively leverage all the data that you collect via these various techniques. We concluded the chapter with a discussion on "strategic timeouts," a method for deep reflection and long-term planning.

Inpowering Leaders increase the accuracy of their decisions by pressure testing them against a variety of inputs and perspectives. They achieve this by building a diverse and engaged talent pool that speaks freely and actively challenges their assumptions. Leaders who operate this way enjoy some unique benefits. Because their teams feel included in the journey, they also feel accountable for outcomes. They are more willing to support unpopular decisions and make difficult choices.

The methods we discussed in this chapter cannot be implemented within a matter of days or even months. *Building a culture of openness and inclusion requires sustained effort – it can take many years to make it part of an organization's DNA.* It is best to waste no time and get going right away. The investments you make today could well be the difference between success and failure when you encounter your next significant disruption.

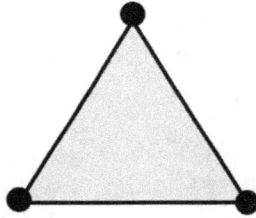

CHAPTER 4 – BUILDING RESILIENCE

A great leader leads the people from within them.

– M. D. Arnold

It was late in the evening, and I was on my way home after a long day at our factory on the outskirts of Bangalore. As my driver navigated the twisty and pothole-ridden roads, I pulled out my phone and made a call to our headquarters in the US. I heard a few rings, and then Ben picked up. I instantly felt better.

Ben Fast[15] was my "functional" supervisor while I was on assignment in India. He was also a mentor and confidant who had advised me as I became a manager

---

[15] Some of the names in this chapter are fictional. The people and anecdotes, however, are real.

and an executive after that.

I had set up today's call because things had been quite tense and hectic at work. My team was toiling hard to deliver several projects on tight timelines. I was personally under immense pressure and needed to vent and process my thoughts.

That night, Ben stayed on the phone with me for over an hour. He listened patiently and made me the center of his attention. He acknowledged the challenges I was facing and then helped me figure out how to get through them.

As always, Ben was there for me in my time of need. He is someone for whom I will always pick up the phone.

Over my career, I had the pleasure of working with some truly inspiring leaders like Ben. All of them were unique in their own ways but had some common elements – they set a positive tone, walked their talk, and always left people feeling more energized after an interaction. They were senior executives under much stress and constantly stretched for time. Even so, they never complained about their own situation, and instead chose to focus on the welfare of the people around them.

These leaders had a growth mindset. With their positive outlook on life, earnest desire to learn, and willingness to invest in people, they created an environment where everyone could thrive and achieve their maximum potential. And when they moved on, they left behind something significantly better than what they had inherited.

In the previous chapters, we discussed techniques for shepherding your organization with purpose, speed, and accuracy through change and disruption. While these techniques are necessary, they are not sufficient. Leading people through change requires more than sound operational tactics; it also requires inspiration. The best leaders know this and operate in ways that inject an extra "oomph" into their people and make them resilient in the face of shocks and disruptions.

In the following sections, I will describe how Inpowering Leaders build resilient organizations that keep going in the face of all odds. These are attributes that I have attempted to emulate and incorporate into my own leadership style.

4.1 INSPIRING AND VISUALIZING SUCCESS

I once worked with a leader who always had a smile on his face when he greeted me. I remember a period when he was going through a lot of professional turmoil. He never let it show even once, however. He was always cheerful, ready to engage, and singularly focused on the mission. When I learned later what he had gone through, I marveled at how he had managed to stay calm through it all.

Inpowering Leaders have an aura of personal belief and optimism. Even in the worst of times, instead of spiraling down a vortex of cynicism and anger, they stay above the fray and actively look for ways to make things better. Their shoulders never droop, and their voice never falters. They jump into each conversation with gusto, putting their personal issues on the back burner, and focusing instead on the people they lead.

About a decade ago, I came across a leadership presentation by Tom Peters that contained the following quote: "It's always showtime!" The unenviable reality for leaders is that they are always on show. Their people look up to them for cues on how things are going. The tone that they set at the top percolates rapidly into the organization.

Times of crisis can severely test the temperament of a team. Great leaders understand this and do everything they can to raise morale and show a path to a better future. They demonstrate support for the mission through visible energy and enthusiasm. When their people come to them with pain, they display empathy and listen patiently. And then they do everything in their power to inspire them to keep moving forward.

Please take a short timeout here and consider the following questions. As you answer them, think about how you can keep your head up when things get rough and inspire everyone around you to keep going.

1. How would your people describe you when it comes to optimism and inspiration? Would they say they look forward to engaging with you? Do

they usually feel uplifted after a conversation with you?

2. Do you make a conscious effort to inspire your people at every touchpoint? When you have hard conversations, do you try to conclude with a positive view of the future?

3. What is your view on this type of leadership? Is it something that you consider important? If yes, what can you do to become more effective? If not, why not?

⧖ **Timeout**

4.2 TEACHING AND MENTORING

I started my career as a research scientist. I joined my company right after completing my Ph.D. and looked forward to continuing where I had left off in grad school.

My first assignment was a helicopter noise control project managed by Matt Danielson, a senior leader with a lot of industry experience. During one of our regular project updates, Matt asked me why I was using a particularly complex mathematical approach to solve the problem. I was quite proud of my work and began to explain it in detail. After listening for a few minutes,

Matt stopped me and asked if there was an easier and more efficient way to get to an answer that was *almost as good*. He then said something that forever changed my approach to problem-solving: "Customers do not care how mathematically elegant your approach is. They only care about how quickly and effectively you solve their problems."

Matt's comment gave me pause. It made me realize that I had become more enamored by the tools of my trade than by the outcomes they created. From then on, I always framed my work through the eyes of my customers.

Leaders like Matt know how to grow people. Even though they are deeply knowledgeable, they resist the temptation to jump in and provide all the answers. They focus instead on creating moments of clarity and encouraging others to figure things out on their own, thus imparting lessons that stick for life.

Leaders like Matt also have a natural talent for demystifying seemingly complex topics. They use analogies and anecdotes to make things more tangible and personal for their listeners. They actively help people understand the complexities of the business by translating them into more understandable language.

Do you remember Ben from the beginning of this chapter? During a project review, he saw that I was having trouble making a business decision. He helped me through it by asking: "Imagine that this was the *Vijay Jayachandran Company*. What would you do?" The way he reframed the problem helped me shift my thinking from that of an employee to that of an owner. It instantly provided clarity and helped me figure out the best path forward. It was a trick I used many times afterward with other people.

Matt and Ben were Inpowering Leaders who willingly invested in the people around them and helped them grow. With every teaching moment, they incrementally built new layers of resilience that would help their organizations survive and thrive well after their departure.

I would like you to pause here and take a timeout. As you answer the following questions, think about your teaching style and your willingness to invest in the people around you.

1. What is your approach to growing and nurturing your people? Do you view every interaction as a potential coaching moment?

2. Can you look back into the last few years and identify the people you have mentored? Are there any that have gone on to become successful leaders in their own right?

3. What is your view on this aspect of leadership? Is this something that you consider important? If yes, what can you do to become more effective? If not, why not?

Timeout

4.3 BEING AVAILABLE AND FULLY PRESENT

Within a year of becoming a manager, I got a new boss – a Vice President named Larry Armando. Larry was a senior leader who I had always admired from a distance. My first interactions with him were cordial. I was, however, still somewhat intimidated by him and not sure how approachable he was.

One day I had a critical issue on a project and wanted to get his input. I walked by his office and saw that his door was open. I mustered my courage, poked my head in, and asked if I could have a few minutes. Larry looked up, smiled, and said: "For you, anytime." I was filled with a mix of surprise and relief. Surprise, because I did not expect Larry to say something as personal as that. And relief because I no longer felt like an intruder. With just three words, he had made me feel welcome into his busy world.

Larry understood how intimidating it was for people like me to approach him and did whatever he could to break down such barriers. He used the power of kind words and gestures to create an environment where people felt comfortable approaching him.

But it did not end there. Once you had Larry's attention, he made himself *fully* available, physically as well as mentally. He indulged you with his time and attention and created a safe space for any type of conversation.

If he could only commit to a short duration, he made it clear at the outset, with a promise that we could always reconvene later if the situation demanded. If he could not meet immediately, he committed to a time when he would be able to speak. And when he finally did sit down with you, he was with you, one hundred percent.

Have you ever worked with leaders who frequently glance at their smartphone or keep stepping out of meetings to take calls from other people? What kind of attention do you think they are paying to what you have to say?

Another leader I worked with, Frank Sansevero, never carried his smartphone with him and instead left it in his office. He told everyone that if they had something urgent to discuss, they could use his calendar to track him down physically. Any requests sent via email or phone would have to wait and be dispositioned during dedicated blocks of time that were set aside expressly for that purpose. Frank's approach allowed him to focus during meetings and fully immerse himself in the conversation taking place.

I admired Frank and learned a lot from observing him. I became quite sensitive to wasting other people's time because of a lack of planning from me. I made every effort to arrive on time, stay focused, and minimize all distractions.

I also developed a rule that no one would ever wait for more than 24 hours to get a response from me for any type of approval. I paid particular attention to requests where people were waiting on me before they could proceed with their work.

By making themselves *fully* available, leaders like Larry and Frank demonstrated respect for the people around them. They inpowered their people by not only providing a place at the table but also showing them that their opinion was heard and valued. Their operating style fostered trust and resulted in more focused and effective interactions[16].

It is time for another quick timeout. As you answer the following questions, think about how you can show respect for other peoples' time and fully immerse yourself in conversations with them.

1. Have you developed any techniques over the years to make people feel at ease when they approach you?

---

[16] A study at the University of California showed that distractions can significantly reduce your output, and that it takes almost 30 minutes to fully get back to focusing on a task after a distraction. Imagine what happens to your focus every time you glance at your phone or step out of a meeting.

2. When people do engage with you, do you fully give them your time and attention? Would people describe you as someone who makes them the center of attention during conversations?

3. Are you someone who multi-tasks during meetings? Do the people around you see you regularly examining your laptop or smart devices? If yes, how do you think they interpret this?

4. What is your view on this aspect of leadership? Is this something that you consider important? If yes, what can you do to become more effective? If not, why not?

Timeout

4.4 DOING THE RIGHT THINGS

Nowadays, almost every company has published a "culture" statement. Leaders in the C-suite have understood the importance of empowerment, diversity, and inclusion for attracting new talent. They have gone into communication overdrive, letting the world know via interviews and social media that these are the values they espouse.

Although vocal support from the top is critical, what really sticks inside an organization are actions. Leaders must show through not only their words but also their actions, that they live by the values they espouse and are genuinely committed to bringing about the changes to which they aspire.

The best leaders I worked with did not talk much about organizational culture. They just went ahead and showed us what they stood for.

When you went to them with a problem, they showed empathy, made a genuine effort to listen, and helped you find a path.

When they empowered you to lead something, they truly stepped back, let you take risks, and played the role of a coach rather than an auditor.

When they included you in a conversation, they ensured that your presence was respected, and your voice was heard.

When they committed to increasing diversity, they made the requisite changes to welcome new entrants and make them feel at home.

That was it. No talk. No drama. Just actions.

Have you worked with people who seem to say all the right things, but you cannot believe their words? I think all of us have had such an experience. After you have worked with people for a reasonable duration, you develop the ability to figure out if they are authentic.

Think back to some of the senior leaders you have worked with, and visualize how you would react if they said, "thank you," "sorry," or "I truly care." Your reaction would likely depend on who said the words.

Words are cheap. Anyone can say them. They are even available as pre-packaged phrases within email and social media apps. Unfortunately, it is not just the words to which we respond. The cumulative actions that precede those words dictate how we feel and react.

People constantly observe their leaders and look for consistency between their actions and their words. The fundamental virtue that I saw in great leaders was that *they always tried to do the right thing*. Both in good times as well as bad. When it was easy and when it was not. Consequences be damned!

Character is about doing the right things even when no one is looking. Every one of us has the innate ability to figure out the right things. The hard part is doing them.

Short-term motivations and constraints can cloud our thinking and take us down alternate paths that seem more expedient and rewarding. That is where great leaders differentiate themselves. They have a strong moral compass that they use to guide their actions, again and again. They initiate hard conversations, push back when inconvenient, and show vulnerability when they need help. They work hard to percolate this mindset all the way to the bottom of their organization. And after they have done it often and long enough, it becomes a part of the organization's DNA.

That, in a nutshell, is how culture is built.

Ben Horowitz, the co-founder of venture-capital firm Andreessen Horowitz, said in a recent interview, "A culture is a set of actions, not beliefs and intents." An organization's culture is not something that can be deliberately designed. It is something organic, an outcome of how they operate over an extended period.

Inpowering Leaders build a culture of doing the right things. They create followers who are willing to go with them anywhere. They are the ones best positioned to succeed in times of change and disruption.

We are now ready for the last timeout in this book. As you answer the following questions, think about the culture you would like to build in your organization and how well you live it every day.

1. Would your people call you authentic? Do they see a correlation between your words and actions? Do they clearly understand who you are and what you stand for?

2. Do you think your people trust you to look out

for them? Do you think they would willingly follow you through thick and thin?

3. What is your brand as a leader? How do you live by it every single day?

4. Do you think your brand might need some adjusting? If yes, what can you do to get there?

Timeout

CHAPTER SUMMARY

In this chapter, we discussed how Inpowering Leaders inspire their people to persevere in difficult times and achieve more than they thought possible.

We discussed behavioral attributes such as showing visible conviction and enthusiasm for the mission, being active mentors and teachers, being fully available during interactions, and always doing the right things – no matter the consequences. These attributes help leaders cement bonds of trust and friendship with their staff and convince them to come along on difficult journeys.

Just imagine how it would feel to lead an energized and engaged army that believes in the mission, moves with purpose, and willingly comes with you towards uncertain horizons. This type of organization will be, by definition, resilient. It will be able to withstand all kinds of systemic shocks and persevere in the face of any disruption or crisis.

Inpowering Leaders leave behind strong and resilient organizations that persist and thrive after they have moved on to new challenges. I hope you will be one of them.

CONCLUDING THOUGHTS

When you get the choice to sit it out or dance, I hope
you dance.

– Lee Ann Womack

Congratulations, my friend, you made it to the end of the book. I hope you had a productive journey and gained some new insights along the way.

In the preceding chapters, I took you on a hands-on journey to learn and apply the four-step Inpowering Leadership framework. We discussed how to:

1. Create a shared sense of *purpose* by aligning the organization towards a common North Star,

2. Increase organizational *speed* by empowering the grassroots and fostering a culture of entrepreneurship,

3. Improve decision-making *accuracy* by building an inclusive and data-centric culture, and

4. Build *resilience* by investing in people and building a culture of doing the right things.

The Inpowering Leadership framework is designed to engage your entire organization and leverage its *inner power* to navigate change and disruption. Executing it will also power your personal growth. Every time you introspect, calibrate, run experiments, and learn, you will stretch yourself along new dimensions and grow as a result.

There is no such thing as a born leader. *Leaders are forged in the crucible of life.*

Most of us are happy to follow the crowd as we pursue happiness and fulfillment. There are some, however, who willingly push themselves out of their comfort zones. They acknowledge their limitations and find ways to overcome them. They continuously look in the mirror and honestly strive to get better. They make mistakes, but then get up, brush themselves off, and start running their next experiment. Before they know it, they reach a tipping point where they have seen enough and experienced enough to be able to get things right most of the time. And that is when they transition to greatness.

All of us have a choice – we can stay static or try something new. The lucky thing is that we do not have to start from scratch. Sir Isaac Newton famously said: "If I have seen further than others, it is by standing upon the shoulders of giants."

Anything meaningful that I achieved during my career was because of the support of leaders and co-workers who placed their faith in me.

Leading others is a privilege. You are responsible for what people get to work on and how fulfilling their everyday journey is. This responsibility gets further amplified in times of change when people start worrying about what the future holds and whether they will have a part in it. As a leader, it is your job to set a clear and inspiring destination for your people and provide them with an honest shot at reaching it.

The most important asset of your organization is your people. It is their creativity and effort that powers your enterprise. Treat them well, lean on them, and include them in the journey. You might be surprised by what you accomplish together.

We are now at the end of our journey. I have given you a bit of myself and hope that you will, in turn, pay it forward to those who look up to you.

If this book helped you in any way, I would love to hear about it. Honest reviews help readers find the right book for their needs.

All that said, what are you waiting for? **GO INPOWER YOUR TEAM!**

EPILOGUE

You take a moment to let your eyes and ears adjust to the noise and glare.

You exchange glances with your fellow warriors. One of them makes the secret sign – he has seen this fearsome creature before. And that is all you need to know. He will take down the animal while the rest will fight the better-known enemy – Roman gladiators.

As the scrimmage unfolds, a calm descends around you. Your team acts as one, fully trusting each other, always listening for cues.

You roar and inspire as you fight alongside your mates and show the way. The battle is over in minutes. You have won!

As you share a round of ale, you look back at what was and what could have been. You strategize, you visualize, you prepare. Because the next one is just around the corner.

Are you ready?

SUGGESTED READINGS

Thinking, Fast and Slow, by Daniel Kahnemann

Evolve Your Brain: The Science of Changing Your Mind, by Joe Dispenza

The Unthinkable: Who Survives When Disaster Strikes – And Why, by Amanda Ripley

Range: Why Generalists Triumph in a Specialized World, by David Epstein

Dance with Chance: Making Luck Work for You, by Spyros Makridakis, Robin Hogarth, Anil Gaba

NOTES

NOTES

NOTES

NOTES

NOTES

NOTES

www.ingramcontent.com/pod-product-compliance
Lightning Source LLC
Chambersburg PA
CBHW031933190326
41519CB00007B/518